XERISCAPE
HANDBOOK

XERISCAPE HANDBOOK

A How-To Guide to
Natural, Resource-Wise Gardening

Gayle Weinstein

FULCRUM PUBLISHING
GOLDEN, COLORADO

Acknowledgments

To my friend and coworker Peter M. Henson, for his friendship, skillful review of the manuscript, and precise computerized illustrations. To my two landscape architect students: Gale Fulton, for his drawings and diligence in interpreting the chapter on design; and Nobuo Iwata, for his beautifully illustrated planting plan. To David Winger at Denver Water and Mike Baron from Rain Bird for their contributions. And mostly to my husband, David, for his encouragement to write and his gentle support when I had doubts. And to my three children, whom I love very much.

Library of Congress Cataloging-in-Publication Data

Weinstein, Gayle.
    Xeriscape handbook : a how-to guide to natural, resource-wise gardening
         p. cm.
    Includes bibliographical references and index.
    ISBN 1-55591-346-6 (pbk.)
    1. Xeriscaping.   I. Title
  SB475.83.W45   1999
  635.9'5—dc21   98-43383
                                                     CIP

Printed in Canada

0 9 8 7 6 5 4 3 2 1

Book design: Jay Staten
Cover design: Beckie Smith
Interior photographs: Gayle Weinstein and Peter M. Henson
Interior illustrations: Gayle Weinstein and Peter M. Henson; Chapter II, Gale Fulton
Cover photo: Charles Mann
Cover illustration: Linda Lorraine Wolfe

Fulcrum Publishing
350 Indiana Street, Suite 350
Golden, Colorado 80401-5093
(800) 992-2908 • (303) 277-1623
website: www.fulcrum-gardening.com

11320 I 5-01

Contents

Introduction, vii

Chapter I: Climate, 1
    Introduction, 1
    Climate, 2

Chapter II: The Design Process, 17
    Phase I: Sensing the Site, 19
    Phase II: Learning or Reviewing the Basics, 21
    Phase III: Initiating the Design on Paper, 21
    Phase IV: Composing the Conceptual Design, 30
    Phase V: Drawing the Final Plan, 56
    Phase VI: Estimating Costs, 56
    Phase VII: Implementing the Plan, 57

Chapter III: Soil, 61
    Getting to Know Your Soil, 64

Chapter IV: Compost, Mulch, and Fertilizer, 81
    Compost, 81
    Mulch, 85
    Fertilizer, 90

Chapter V: Planting and Development, Health, and Maintenance, 97
    Planting, 97
    Plant Development, Health, and Maintenance, 103

Chapter VI: Applying Water, 115
    Irrigation, 115
    Water Harvesting, 124
    Recycled Water (Gray Water), 126

Glossary, 129
Bibliography, 136
Index, 137

Introduction

It has been my goal to find ways of creating a functional, pleasing, yet easily maintained landscape that complements its natural surroundings. A landscape that fits in with the environment, neither robbing it of its natural beauty and resources nor working against the forces of nature. A design that is fulfilling and also sustainable. One that is practical and planned with common sense. A landscape that is holistic, healthy, and responsive to semiarid and arid environments.

This book focuses on five major concepts:
1. Growing and enjoying plants in a semi-arid to arid region
2. Conserving our natural resources in the landscape and garden
3. Creating an awareness of the natural environment
4. Developing a compatible alliance among the garden, landscape, and natural world
5. Applying the seven basic principles of xeriscape

1. Growing and Enjoying Plants in a Semiarid to Arid Region

Growing plants in drier climates can be both challenging and frustrating. In some cases, to be successful, time-honored gardening practices may need to be reevaluated. This book sorts out—and, in some cases, revises and challenges—some of these practices and landscape maintenance routines in order to address today's issues about preserving the environment and encouraging the conservation of our natural resources.

2. Conserving Our Natural Resources in the Landscape and Garden

We live in a country rich in natural resources and opportunities. Some, such as water and soil, are critical to gardening and landscapes. As populations grow, development and consumerism increase, placing greater demands on these resources. Supplies and opportunities shrink. As a consequence, we have to work harder to maintain the lifestyles we have long enjoyed. However, if we change the way we do things and take better care of our resources, we can make them last longer, and enjoy more options. In this handbook, in order to encourage conservation, basic design principles incorporate the added dimensions of climate, regional weather conditions, microclimates, soil, water, and plant relationships.

3. Creating an Awareness of the Natural Environment

The trend in gardening and landscaping has often been to ignore natural conditions. If we continue to do so, however, it will create greater problems for our generation and most assuredly for the generations to follow. By focusing on an awareness of our natural ecological systems, we can integrate some of their processes into our gardens and landscapes, and, ideally, become more cognizant, responsible, and less wasteful of our resources. Ultimately, we may all gain a greater appreciation of the natural world.

4. Developing a Compatible Alliance Among the Garden, Landscape, and Natural World

People move around. When they do, they bring past comforts with them to ease their reestablishment. Within a building or home, it is relatively easy to safeguard such personal treasures as furniture, pictures, and knickknacks because the climate can be controlled. The outside landscape may be much more difficult. Moving and growing plants from humid environments (such as New England or the Pacific Northwest) to the semiarid or arid environments of the High Plains grasslands, arid shrub lands, or southwestern deserts, where climates are considerably drier, overburdens natural resources. Landscapes native to humid environments (30 to 40 inches of precipitation per year) transplanted to the arid West (4 to 15 inches of rainfall) may more than double water use. The rainfall amount in an area is crucial for determining what can grow naturally as well as the amount of water that must be used for irrigation. It takes approximately 700 gallons a day to maintain the same landscape in the arid West that requires 400 to 500 gallons a day in the more humid East. But rainfall is not the only consideration. Low relative humidity, ultraviolet radiation, and desiccating winds are also contributing factors. Mimicking designs and gardening practices, and using plants commonly grown in humid regions in more arid areas is not only inappropriate, but wasteful. On the other hand, taking into account the natural environment and local climate will result in landscapes that will conserve and preserve our natural resources and the region's inherent beauty. Benefiting ourselves as well as future generations, we can reconnect with nature through our own backyards.

5. Applying the Seven Basic Principles of Xeriscape

The principles of xeriscape are based on planning and common sense. They include:

- Developing a landscape design plan— one that integrates irrigation and maintenance into the design/planning process
- Reducing turf and high-water-use areas
- Using a sensible approach to soil improvement with amendments or aeration
- Selecting appropriate plants for the site
- Mulching the soil to reduce evaporative water loss and protect against erosion

- Irrigating efficiently and employing sound watering practices
- Setting up a maintenance program that not only preserves the integrity of the design, but is efficient in its use of resources

This *Xeriscape Handbook* is divided into six major chapters. Chapter I discusses climate and the environment in relationship to the landscape. Understanding the regional climate and local weather patterns helps you to better appreciate why the region is as it is, and is essential for designing and maintaining a xeriscape landscape. The effects of sun, rain, and temperature in the landscape influence plant growth and determine growth requirements. Chapter II focuses on design as a step-by-step process that aids in formulating a new design or retrofitting all parts of an already established one. Chapters III and IV provide information on soil, soil improvement, and protection. Soil is an often overlooked natural resource, and understanding its composition will support your landscape decisions. Chapter V highlights planting and plant development, health, and maintenance. Once you understand how plants grow and what nourishes growth, it is easier to care for them in the landscape. Chapter VI summarizes irrigation methods and offers practical ways to conserve water.

As you read and work through the *Xeriscape Handbook*, it is my hope that you will feel a sense of accomplishment, create a pleasing, comfortable landscape design, and acquire a heightened appreciation for the natural world. Good luck.

Xeriscape strengthens an appreciation for the natural world.

CHAPTER I

Climate

Introduction

If this chapter were a play, it would encompass characters, events, and a story line. In some respects, that's exactly what it is. The characters are the elements of climate; the events are the interactions between and influences of the elements; and the story line is the environmental consequences of these interactions. In this chapter, the stage is set with the discussion of climate and its influence. Your response will ultimately take the form of your own xeriscape landscape design. It would be unrealistic to try to create a successful xeriscape design without considering the local climate and the natural environment.

This is an era of environmental consciousness. Not only are we concerned about water and air quality, but we are also beginning to pay attention to our wealth of natural resources and how we consume them, especially water. These considerations can change attitudes and present new challenges for how we landscape (*Figure 1.1*). The way to meet them is to be informed—be attentive, learn more about the natural world, and respect and work with it.

Have you ever scanned the first few pages of an atlas? Figure 1.2 illustrates how throughout the world there are similar environments and distinctive "vegetative expressions" that develop under similar climatic conditions. These vegetative expressions include forests, grasslands, shrub lands, deserts, and tundra. It is from these areas that many of our landscape plants originate. The same regional conditions affect the local

Figure 1.1—Our natural semiarid prairies and deserts (background) are frequently changed to a higher water use landscape.

It would be ideal if housing developments, parks, and residential areas were designed with the natural environment in mind. Conserving water would be easier and our landscapes wouldn't require as many resources for their maintenance.

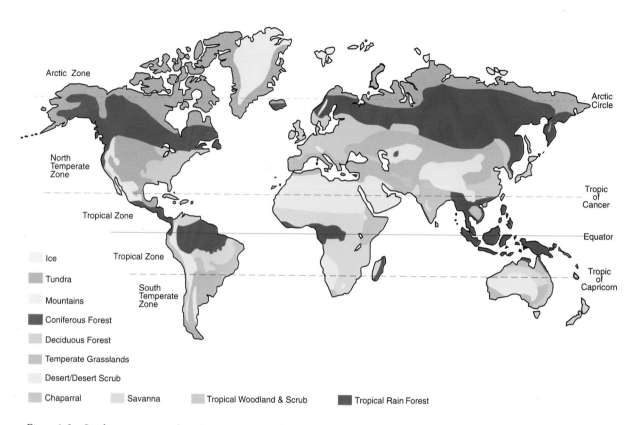

Arctic Zone

Arctic Circle

North Temperate Zone

Tropic of Cancer

Tropical Zone

Equator

Tropical Zone

Ice

South Temperate Zone

Tropic of Capricorn

Tundra

Mountains

Coniferous Forest

Deciduous Forest

Temperate Grasslands

Desert/Desert Scrub

Chaparral   Savanna   Tropical Woodland & Scrub   Tropical Rain Forest

Figure 1.2—Similar environmental conditions provide similar types of vegetation throughout the world.

landscape and plant performance. If you understand them, you can make better choices for your design and plant selections. That is, if you design with an awareness of the regional climate and select plants from areas similar to those of your local natural environment, then you can reduce your use of water, fertilizers, pesticides, and time. For example, growing trees in an area that was once a forest (prior to development) requires fewer resources than growing trees in an area that was once grassland or desert. By understanding the climatic conditions and soil type that produce a forest, you are better prepared to create an environment that favors trees in the urban landscape. (Trees are used as the example because they are the dominant feature of our landscapes, parks, and cityscapes, but the same holds true for other plant forms.)

Climate

Climate is what gives an area its unique personality. Deserts are deserts, prairies are prairies, and forests are forests largely due to climate. We often choose to live where we like the climate. A sensitive landscape designer looks to the local climate for clues. As you plan your xeriscape, it is to your advantage to consider all the components that make up the climate where you live and how the climate will affect your site. These components include solar radiation (sunshine), temperature, precipitation, relative humidity, and wind.

SOLAR RADIATION

Throughout the world, solar radiation and latitude influence the amount of heat energy that

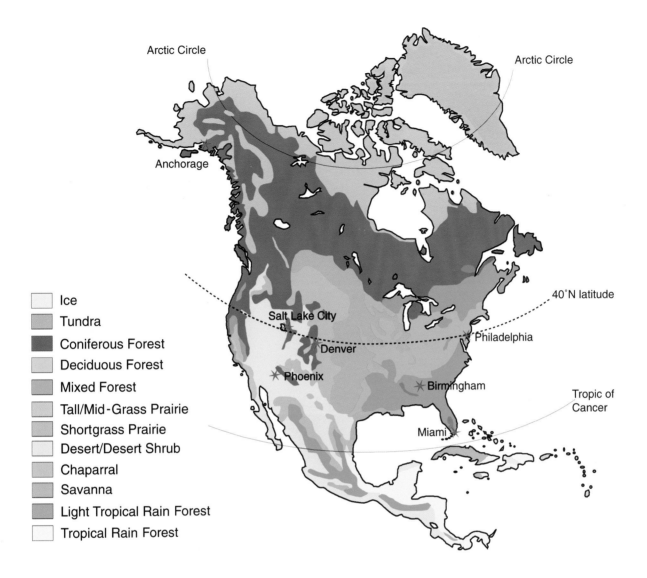

Legend:
- Ice
- Tundra
- Coniferous Forest
- Deciduous Forest
- Mixed Forest
- Tall/Mid-Grass Prairie
- Shortgrass Prairie
- Desert/Desert Shrub
- Chaparral
- Savanna
- Light Tropical Rain Forest
- Tropical Rain Forest

City	Latitude	Average temperature (°F)	Precipitation (inches)	Sunny/cloudy days	Percent sun reaching earth on sunny day	Vegetation
Anchorage	61.10° N	35.9	15.91	60/241	41%	Coniferous forest
Birmingham	33.30° N	61.8	59.58	99/155	58%	Mixed forest
Denver	39.45° N	50.3	15.40	115/120	69%	Short/mid-grass prairie
Miami	25.45° N	72.5	55.91	74/115	69%	Mixed forest
Philadelphia	40.00° N	54.3	41.41	93/160	56%	Deciduous forest
Phoenix	33.50° N	72.6	7.66	211/70	85%	Warm desert
Salt Lake City	40.45° N	52.0	16.18	125/139	67%	Cold desert

Figure 1.3—Solar radiation and latitude strongly influence temperature, relative humidity, precipitation, and resulting vegetation.

builds up in the various regions (*Figure 1.3*). As the sun's rays strike the earth, the earth warms, causing an increase in temperature and, in turn, affecting relative humidity, evaporation, and soil moisture. What happens to the heat that accumulates during the day constitutes the major difference between humid areas (where forests develop) and arid to semiarid climates (where deserts and grasslands develop). In humid environments, by late evening, cloud cover prevents much of the heat from radiating out, resulting in a small temperature difference between day and night. On the other hand, in more arid areas, heat is not retained by cloud cover, and when evening comes, temperatures drop, creating a wide temperature gap between day and night. Day to night temperature ranges say a lot about an area. If the temperature range is minimal, it is usually due to many cloudy days, adequate precipitation throughout the year, and high relative humidity. The many plants that naturally grow in this environment usually require moist soil. If the range is wide, it usually means many sunny days, seasonal or low precipitation, and low relative humidity. The plants that naturally grow in this environment tolerate full sun, low relative humidity, and seasonally drier soil. Areas exhibiting the narrowest daily temperature range are generally situated near large bodies of water such as oceans and lakes (water modifies the effects of temperature). Areas with more extreme daily temperature ranges include mountain valleys where there is significant evening heat loss on clear nights or warm areas that receive the greatest amount of radiation, such as parts of Arizona, California, Colorado, New Mexico, Nevada, and Utah.

Solar energy and light are critical to the landscape. Depending on latitude and compass direction, light creates sun and shade patterns that significantly affect soil, temperature, moisture, irrigation, plant growth, and human comfort. The more direct and longer the sun strikes an area, the warmer the area becomes and the greater is the difference between sunny and shaded areas. A shaded area may be 10–15°F cooler, more humid, or darker than the area in the sun. This difference is even more pronounced at high elevations where sunny areas feel very warm, but in the shade it is quite cool.

Slopes are also affected; north-facing slopes receive less radiation and are cooler than south-facing ones. At ground level, the amount of solar-radiated heat is influenced by the color and exposure of the soil and other surfaces. Lighter, more exposed surfaces reflect heat, raising the surrounding air temperature; darker, less open surfaces absorb the heat. On a sunny day, walk through your landscape and note the areas of sun and shade and how different they feel. These areas illustrate some of the microclimates you will focus on later when designing your plan.

Light is also vital to plant growth. Its presence or absence may determine whether seeds germinate or not. Once seeds germinate, they immediately respond to light. Roots grow down, stems grow up, and as they emerge from the soil, they begin to utilize light in photosynthesis (manufacturing simple sugars). The plant continues to grow and develop depending on light as its source of energy, acquiring new leaves and stems until it flowers. In some plants, the amount of light determines if they will flower. Plants such as chrysanthemum and strawberries need short days and long nights; many ornamental shrubs need shorter nights and longer days; still others are neutral—the length of the day has no effect (*Figure 1.4*).

Light also affects the storage of nutrients. The more sugars a plant manufactures, the more it is likely to store. Storage of nutrients is important to a plant's resistance and its ability to recover from drought, cold temperatures, insect attack, or other stress.

Light influences cell arrangement or the types of leaves produced—that is, sun or shade leaves. Plants adapted to more humid, shady environments tend to have thinner, larger leaves than those adapted to full sun in arid environments.

Leaves that normally flourish in shade will become pale or scorched when exposed to full sunlight. Plants thriving in full sun may defoliate when placed in shade for any length of time.

Sunlight is not only critical to plant growth, it also activates seasonal change and dormancy. In the temperate zone, it is the shorter days and different wavelengths of light that alter a plant's physiology for winter. Leaves begin to change—they stop growing, lose moisture, and lose or turn color before falling. At the same time, buds develop for next year's growth. Once this occurs, the plant is considered to be dormant (in a resting stage) and cold temperature hardy. In the cityscape, artificial night lighting can prevent some plants from going dormant. Sensitive species such as maple, birch, catalpa, and elm growing near night lights may react to inaccurate signals and

Figure 1.4—Plants are more compact in full sun (left) and leggier in shade (right).

continue to grow until they are injured by frosts. Many animals and insects also respond to artificial night lights. Nocturnal animals may be confused and night-flying insects may be attracted to feed on plants adjacent to the lights.

TEMPERATURE

Temperature is closely tied to solar radiation and latitude. The more direct the sun's rays, the greater the light intensity; the greater the intensity, the warmer the temperature. That is why it is warmer near the equator at low latitudes and colder near the poles at high latitudes.

In the natural world, temperatures set parameters for where plants (and animals) live and migrate. For example, needle evergreens (fir and spruce) naturally grow at high latitudes or high elevations where temperatures dip below freezing, but many broadleaf evergreens such as schefflera or fig naturally prefer lower latitudes where it never freezes (*Figure 1.5*).

PLANT HARDINESS

In cultivation, one of the first questions asked about a plant has to do with temperature. Is it hardy? Temperature hardiness is based on the average-low winter temperatures. Temperature is so important in agriculture that the United States Department of Agriculture developed a hardiness zone map for agricultural crops (*Figure 1.6*). North America is divided into 10-de-gree increments representing average-low winter temperatures. These constitute hardiness zones. Plant temperature hardiness is determined by the coldest temperature a plant can survive without disrupting or damaging its life cycle, tissues, growth, or development. Hardiness zone maps were later adapted for ornamental plants and now several versions are available. Most garden catalogs and plant books refer to these zones; make sure you note which map is being used as their frame of reference.

Figure 1.5—Needle evergreens (conifers) naturally grow at high elevation and high latitude.

Figure 1.6—USDA Plant Hardiness Zone Map.

Temperature hardiness zones provide viable guidelines, but cold is not the only factor in plant performance. Other factors, either directly or indirectly, determine a plant's overall hardiness. These include water stress, relative humidity, evaporation rates, wind, elevation, nutrition, and soil composition. Furthermore, hardiness does not apply uniformly to all plant parts. Plant tissues and organs (bark, growing tissue, buds, leaves, flowers, roots, and stems) differ in their response to temperature depending on location, tissue maturity, time of year, and previous fruit, flower, and foliage load. Flower buds on forsythia, magnolia, and apricot may be killed by an early frost even though the rest of the plant thrives *(Figure 1.7)*.

Generally, roots are not as cold hardy as stems and branches. Their hardiness commonly

Figure 1.7—*Magnolia flowers damaged by early freeze.*

relates to soil moisture content. They are sometimes killed or injured even though the tops are unharmed. Plants growing in above-ground containers or planters with less soil volume have less insulation and should be selected for a lower hardiness zone than normal. Also, fruit or nut varieties are sometimes hardier than the rootstocks on which they are grafted (or vice versa).

What temperature hardiness zone are you in? What other areas of the country or world have temperature conditions similar to your area? How do these areas differ from where you live? Your region may have the same temperature zone as another, but the natural vegetation may be quite different. (Precipitation and soil are also factors to consider.) Look at nurseries and garden catalogs for plants within your hardiness zone. Are any of them native to your region?

HARDENING OFF
Temperate zone plants from mid-latitudes have the ability to harden or acclimate to cold temperatures. This means they can physiologically change from a susceptible (tender) condition of summer to a resistant (hardy) one of winter. Acclimation to cold is usually triggered by shorter days and cooler temperatures, causing a general decrease in growth activity. There are four periods when plants may sustain temperature injury because they lose hardiness or are not hardened enough. (1) In the fall, some plants from different regions do not stop growing and fail to mature before freezing weather sets in. This is because environmental conditions do not correspond with the plant's internal biological clock. For example, many bedding plants (e.g., tomato) will grow until killed by a freeze. In some cases, trees and shrubs physiologically move through the stages of dormancy, but because of erratic temperature changes (not infrequent in semiarid areas), the hardening off process is interrupted, leaving the plant unprotected. (2) In winter, injury may result from temperatures dropping below a plant's minimal survival point. This is common when there is a rapid change from day to night temperatures and little evening cloud cover. Parts most often injured are bark, twigs, or buds. Such plants may be borderline in their hardiness. (3) Injury can occur in late winter or early spring when temperatures are cold, sunlight is intense, and winds are chilling. This is often the case at higher elevations where low relative humidity results in desiccation of evergreen needles/leaves, bark, or stems. (4) Injury is also possible in spring if plants break dormancy too early because of unexpected warm spells. When we take species that are native to southern temperate latitudes and plant them farther north, or when we cultivate plants from milder climates with briefer chilling requirements, they are more susceptible in areas with shorter growing seasons—pears, cherries, and apricots are a few examples.

Symptoms of cold injury include wilting, blackened foliage, twigs, flowers and fruit, dieback, defoliation of evergreens, or death.

To avoid these problems, choose plants with hardier characteristics or plant tender varieties in protected areas (microclimates) of the landscape.

GROWING SEASONS
In cultivation, temperature and plant growth relate directly to growing seasons. The growing

TABLE 1.1

Plant type	Minimum Temperature °F	Maximum Temperature °F	Optimum Temperature °F
tundra zone plants	32	86	50
temperate zone plants	40	105	77–86
tropical zone plants	50	122	86–95

season is defined as the period between the last frost of spring and the first frost of autumn. It is, presumably, the time when plants can grow without danger of frost. Plants are evaluated based on how freezing temperatures affect them. A light freeze between 29–32°F kills tender plants such as tomatoes, but inflicts minimal damage on others. A moderate freeze encompasses 25–28°F and damages most vegetation and all flowers and fruits. A severe or hard freeze—below 24°F—causes extensive damage to most plants. Because other factors also influence a plant's temperature requirements, a quantified growing season can sometimes be misleading. Many perennials renew growth before the growing season even starts.

CARDINAL TEMPERATURES

Cardinal temperatures refer to the minimum cold, maximum hot, and ideal ranges for a given plant's growth and development. These temperatures vary among species, but can be generalized for types. For example, cardinal temperatures for tundra plants (those that grow above tree line) extend from 32–86°F, with the optimum at around 50°F. Temperate zone plant ranges extend from 40–105°F with the optimum falling between 77–86°F. Tropical plants range from 50–122°F with their optimum between 86–95°F. A plant's temperature range may vary with its stage of growth. Plants in a dormant state or those growing very slowly can endure higher or lower temperatures. For example, needleleaf evergreens (such as spruce or fir) in winter can

tolerate -60–-70°F, yet, 25–30°F can be fatal once they are actively growing. Although all plants have their cardinal range, plant parts can differ from one another. This is one reason why a plant may grow well, but never flower because its flower buds never reached the needed temperature. An example is apricot, very adaptable to cultivation in a wide range of climates, but it rarely flowers or fruits where freezing temperatures extend into May. If it does flower, the flowers are often damaged.

Plants cultivated in areas where they are subjected to their maximum hot and minimum cold temperatures (natural survival range) get pushed to the limits of their endurance. They may never acclimate or they may break dormancy early. If plants originating from warmer climates or lower elevations are grown in colder climates or at higher latitudes, they may never fully develop buds, flowers, or fruit. If plants have evolved at lower latitudes, but are transplanted to higher latitudes or elevations, they may continue to grow until interrupted or damaged by frosts—they don't harden off, and just one stressful event may prove fatal. Or stress may accumulate and present itself a year or more later. When a tree or shrub dies without apparent reason, it may be due to stress experienced one or several seasons earlier.

High temperatures can be equally as injurious as cold temperatures. High temperatures, like light intensity, increase internal moisture loss. Stunting, deformity, defoliation, poor or no flower, fruit, or seed production are the results.

Figure 1.8—Aspens growing at 5,000 feet in elevation show signs of stress.

Stress also increases a plant's susceptibility to pests, diseases, and climate changes. Birch and aspen naturally grow at higher latitudes or elevations. When they are cultivated in warmer environments, stretching their cardinal range, they are short-lived, vulnerable to more pest and disease problems (*Figure 1.8*).

Generally, plants, like animals, do what they need to do to survive. If threatened, they will divert their efforts toward protection and survival rather than growth. Because this requires a lot of internal energy, healthy plants have a better chance of surviving stress. The more similar the growing conditions are to the plant's natural environment, the more likely the plant will be healthy in cultivation. *Note: In 1997 the American Horticultural Society announced the release of a heat-zone map. It consists of twelve zones indicating the average number of days a region experiences temperatures above 86°F-heat days. (Eighty-six degrees is the boundary because, on average, plant proteins begin to break down at this temperature.) Soon, plants will not only be categorized by temperature hardiness zones, but also by their heat zones. This may prove to be more useful in semiarid and arid climates than hardiness zones.*

PRECIPITATION AND HUMIDITY

Precipitation is any visible moisture that falls to the ground. We see it as rain, snow, sleet, or hail. It is measured in inches or centimeters. Humidity is the invisible moisture we feel in the air. It is expressed as a percentage because it is based on the maximum quantity of water vapor the air can hold at the prevailing temperature. An area with high precipitation and high relative humidity is considered humid. An area with low precipitation and low relative humidity is considered arid.

Humidity and aridity are relative terms. Rainforests are the most humid environs. They exhibit a daily low relative humidity around 80 percent and annual precipitation well over 60 inches. Deserts are the most arid environs. Their average daily low relative humidity is 10 percent with precipitation less than 12 inches per year. Grasslands are the transitional zones between semiarid to subhumid. Humid areas receive enough precipitation to replace soil moisture, and the excess replenishes groundwater. Arid areas net insufficient precipitation to continuously replace soil moisture and only rarely

is there any excess to restore groundwater. In humid to semiarid areas, precipitation generally falls in sufficient amounts during the plant's growing season when it can use it. In more arid areas, precipitation may come during the growing season, accompany dormancy, or may not occur at all. Which environment is most like yours?

Most plants used in the traditional landscape come from humid environments. When we attempt to cultivate these plants in drier regions, they require a lot more water—more water in an area with less than 10–15 inches of rainfall a year and 10–20 percent relative humidity can be a significant amount.

PLANTS AND HUMIDITY

Water is critical to the character of a region and the plants that grow there. Although there are plants that live *in* water (e.g., water lilies) with a ready supply and there are those that receive moisture from the air (many orchids), most plants live on land (terrestrial) and rely on moisture from precipitation (or irrigation) via the soil. The path water follows in a plant is to first travel through its roots (absorption). It then moves up through the stems to the leaves. During this process, the plant uses what it needs (about 5 percent) and the rest is ultimately transpired back into the atmosphere through leaf openings called stomates (*Figure 1.9*). The rate at which water moves through the plant depends on the disparity between the amount of water in the soil and in the air. If the soil is moist and the air is dry, water movement and water loss (transpiration) is high. If the relative humidity is high, transpiration is less. Dry soil combined with low relative humidity (common conditions of semiarid and arid areas) predispose plants to water stress.

Many plants can tolerate high transpiration rates as long as their roots are supplied with water. In general, low relative humidity is less critical to plant growth than dry soil. As long as irrigation is an option (other things being equal), it is fairly easy to cultivate plants from humid environments in more arid ones, but is this a wise use of water? There are some species that suffer as a result of low relative humidity regardless of soil moisture content. Many of these plants exhibit very thin foliage such as Japanese maple and maidenhair fern.

DROUGHT AND DRYNESS

"Drought" and "dryness" are two commonly used terms that sound similar but are actually quite different. Drought is a meteorological term referring to a lack of rainfall, which is normal for arid and semiarid regions. Dryness is a relative term describing water deficits that may be more frequent, more severe, or longer lasting than "normal." Dryness can result from soil compaction, poor soil structure, and runoff. Both drought and dryness can negatively affect plant growth. Outward signs of water stress are wilt, shrinking of stem tissue, discolored or distorted leaves, early fall color, premature leaf drop, cracks, twigs and stem dieback, and straggly growth. Dry soil and drought are common in all areas.

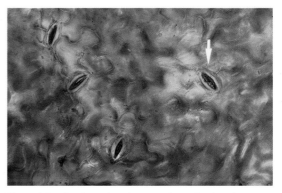

Figure 1.9—Leaf openings (stomates) are the site of transpiration and gas exchange.

In humid areas, native plants make very efficient use of water when it is available. They grow more quickly and are able to store food for leaner times; however, a short, dry period may be devastating—more so than native plants enduring a long period of drought in semiarid to arid environments. This is due, in part, because plants in drier environments have evolved and adapted to less precipitation and lower humidity. Adaptations take the form of small leaves, waxy coatings, and thick cuticles that help retard internal water loss (*Figure 1.10*). Unlike plants from humid environments, many dryland plants are not very efficient as they grow very slowly even when water is available. Regardless, a plant's water needs—whether in its natural environment or in cultivation—are based on what it takes to keep it alive.

Figure 1.10—Some plant adaptations to drier climates include small leaves, thick cuticles, and hairy coverings.

WIND

Wind is air in motion. Sometimes it is gentle, other times it is harsh. Nonetheless, it moves clouds and fog, changes air temperature, fashions snowfall into drifts, and leaves some areas bare and dry. Wind removes moisture from the air and plant cells, transports soil and airborne particles, disperses seeds long distances, and fans fires far beyond their origins. Harsh winds are capable of causing severe plant damage, deformity, or breakage and play a dominant role in water loss (*Figure 1.11*). They are capable of drying out seedlings in only minutes, young transplants in hours, and soil in one day. Winds also alter temperature. A 15-mph wind can lower cold air temperatures by 30°F within a few hours.

Wind speed over land depends on topography, barriers, and vegetation. Obstacles such as buildings, mountains, trees, and hedges can alter the wind's direction and speed. At high elevations atop hills, mountains, and buildings, wind is intensified. Across vast open spaces, winds can blow without restraint. Winds usually flow downhill and can then be trapped, forming pockets of warm or cold air, typical in mountain valleys.

Figure 1.11—High winds at high elevation cause plant deformities.

From what direction do your prevailing winds come? At what time of year? Where is the most exposed area of your site? Where is the most sheltered area? In your landscape design, you can minimize the effects of wind by planting barriers or windbreaks that alter or slow its course. Solid barriers will divert the wind over and around their edges; filtered windbreaks or barriers will slow it down.

TOPOGRAPHY

Up to now, we have been looking at climate as if the earth were flat. However, the topography or surface features of an area modify climate and create microclimates. Slopes and mountain ranges, large bodies of water such as oceans and lakes, and large land masses create their own microclimates. Areas near water tend to be mild and humid. Areas not surrounded by large bodies of water tend to be colder in winter and hotter in summer. Mountains constitute major barriers—they block air movement and influence winds, precipitation, humidity, and evaporation (*Figure 1.12*).

If the land is sloping, its exposure—that is, the direction it faces—affects climate. The windward side may receive more precipitation, leaving the leeward side in a rain shadow. The

Figure 1.12—Areas near large bodies of water tend to be more humid.

eastern side of the Rocky Mountains may experience warm Chinook winter winds, raising temperatures to 50°F and quickly evaporating any snow cover. Slopes that face south and southwest receive more direct, intense sun comprising warmer areas with different vegetation from those that face north and northeast. Because of the warmer temperatures, spring comes earlier to a south slope than a north slope.

Slope elevations, clear, thin air, and low relative humidity contribute to a dramatic contrast between sun and shaded areas. This may translate to short-sleeved shirts in sun and jackets in shade. Nights at higher elevations are much cooler than at lower elevations of the same latitude. Growing seasons also shorten as elevation increases because frosts arrive earlier and stay later. However, cool nights may be the limiting factor for plant development and fruiting rather than the length of the growing season. Eggplant and tomatoes are two examples. Microclimates change with elevation. An increase in elevation means a decrease in temperature but an increase in precipitation. In general, a 300-foot gain in elevation is equivalent to a one-degree increase in latitude. One thousand feet in elevation roughly equals 600 miles plus or minus in latitude. For every 1,000 feet in elevation, there is a 3.5–5.5°F temperature difference. Plant development, bloom time, and fruit production correlate to latitude and altitude. To find the season you just missed, go north in latitude or climb in elevation (*Figure 1.13 on page 12*).

PLANTS AND CLIMATE

Over time, plants adapt and evolve with the natural environment. Collectively, they become signifiers of environmental conditions. Some areas develop into forests dominated by trees; others become prairies dominated by grasses, and still others comprise deserts or wetlands. A major factor in determining why plants grow in wet, moist, or dry conditions is their ability to adapt to water availability. For example, plants that grow in water or saturated soil (called "hydrophytes"), such as water lilies, cattails, and willows, in the natural environment are hallmarks of wetlands.

xerophyte

Figure 1.14—Comparison of a hydrophyte (cattail), mesophyte (maple), and xerophyte (fernbush).

mesophyte

hydrophyte

Many of these plants will also flourish in a landscape where similar wet conditions are duplicated. Adding these plants can potentially offer a solution to such problem areas as standing water

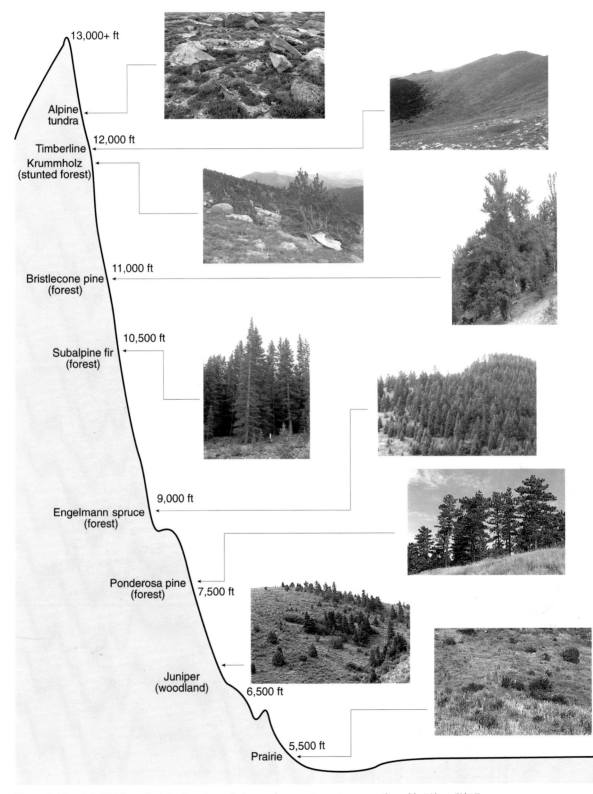

13,000+ ft

Alpine
tundra

12,000 ft

Timberline

Krummholz
(stunted forest)

11,000 ft

Bristlecone pine
(forest)

10,500 ft

Subalpine fir
(forest)

9,000 ft

Engelmann spruce
(forest)

Ponderosa pine
(forest)

7,500 ft

Juniper
(woodland)

6,500 ft

5,500 ft

Prairie

Figure 1.13—A 1,000-foot climb in elevation will show a decrease in temperature of roughly $3\frac{1}{2}$ to $5\frac{1}{2}$°F.

or high water tables, poor soil drainage or wet areas due to runoff, and excessive irrigation.

"Xerophytes"—the counterpoint of hydrophytes—are dryland plants adapted to areas of low relative humidity, low precipitation, and dry soil. Cacti, many grasses, succulents, and certain shrubs are the dominant plant forms generally found in prairies, shrub lands, deserts, and open woodlands. In the landscape, these plants are ideal for areas where water drains quickly such as on steep slopes, in gravelly or sandy soil, on western or southern exposures, and near reflected heat where a low-water-use landscape is desired.

The third type of plants classified by water adaptation consists of the "mesophytes." These thrive where moisture is available year-round and cannot survive excessively wet or overly dry soil. Mesophytes are the most commonly used plants in the landscapes of temperate North America, Europe, and Asia. They include maples, oaks, beech, elm, hackberry, lindens, forsythia, lilacs, and many more. To establish mesophytes in regions with low relative humidity and limited natural precipitation, supplemental irrigation and usually soil amendments will be necessary (*Figure 1.14*).

IDEAS FROM NATURE FOR SEMIARID AND ARID LANDSCAPES

Because forests, grasslands, and deserts constitute major natural vegetative covers, they and the transitional areas that develop between them provide excellent sources of plants and ideas for landscape designs.

Parklands are combinations of trees and grass. They differ from true forests because trees are spaced far enough apart that the canopies do not touch, enabling the sun to penetrate to the ground below. Natural precipitation in these areas is more seasonal and more limited than in a forest. Trees may be evergreen as in areas in the central valley of California, with live oaks or pines and bunchgrasses in the mountain foothills, or they may be deciduous such as the eastern edge of the mid-grass prairie and where bur oak and grasses merge. Because parklands encompass trees and grass—the two dominant features in man-made landscapes—the combination offers design solutions for semiarid landscapes (*Figure 1.15*).

Woodlands are also open forests, with a variety of widely spaced small-stature trees. They occur naturally in areas that are warm enough to support forests, but at elevations low enough that drought can be a problem. Most woodlands receive 15–25 inches of precipitation per year, primarily in the winter. Woodlands are typical of the

Figure 1.15—Parkland and savannas encompass trees and grass, two dominant features of man-made landscapes.

intermountain regions between the Sierra Nevada and the Rocky Mountains. They also form a distinct natural zone in the southern Rockies. Dominant species include juniper, piñon, and Arizona cypress between 10 to 30 feet tall. This western type of forest is often nicknamed "pygmy forest." (*Figure 1.16*). Open spaces between trees support grasses, some shrubs, and herbaceous plants. In the natural environment, open woodlands are usually transition zones between desert shrub land or grassland and mountain forests. In these woodlands, an increase in elevation brings an increase in the density of trees that eventually merge into forests, and species change. This vegetation is characteristic of foothills, plateaus,

Figure 1.16—Open woodlands consist of widely spaced, small-statured trees such as junipers and piñon pines (above).

Prairie grasslands also contribute ideas for xeriscape landscapes. The powerful combination of wildflowers and grasses not only offers ever-changing scenes, but also provides gratifying ways to transform a traditional lawn to a prairie or meadow landscape (*Figure 1.18*).

Figure 1.17—Shrub lands are often found in areas too dry for trees. Plants may include manzanita, mountain mahogany, and sage (left).

Figure 1.18—Prairie grasslands provide a powerful combination of wildflowers and grasses (below).

mesas, and canyons. The combination of plants and the way they are organized along with rock and stone outcroppings suggest many possibilities and ideas for landscaping semiarid and arid environments. The shrub lands, dominated by shrubs 3 to 18 feet tall, are usually adjacent to woodlands. They develop in areas with 5–12 inches of annual precipitation, often replacing forests where sites are too dry. Shrub lands disclose practical ideas for borders, hedges, screens, and windbreaks (*Figure 1.17*).

WHAT ARE YOUR LOCAL CLIMATIC CONDITIONS?

(For the following information, you can check with your local weather station, cooperative extension, or the Internet.)

- What is the average precipitation of your area?
- When does most of the precipitation come?
- Does the precipitation come as rain or snow?
- What is the wettest month?
- What is the driest month?
- What is the average relative humidity of your area?
- In what month is the relative humidity highest? When is it lowest?

- What is the temperature range?
- What is the coldest month? The hottest month?
- What is the growing season for your area?
- What is the average number of sunny days?
- How strong are the winds?
- From what direction do the prevailing winds for each season come?
- When are winds most powerful and potentially most destructive?

CHAPTER II

The Design Process

Think of xeriscaping as an adventure—like going somewhere for the first time, leaving preconceived notions of landscape and gardening behind. Briefly reflect and imagine the land before it was developed. Was it prairie, forest, shrub land or desert? What types of animals lived there and why? Did it support trees everywhere or just along the streams? What was the rainfall or snowfall like? How did the land sustain itself without irrigation, without fertilizer, and without humans?

The land (your site) has changed since people came onboard and the question is—what is it capable of now? Can a hint of the natural environment, its past, be reintroduced? You ask, why? The intent of the *Xeriscape Handbook* is to introduce water conservation and some natural processes back into the landscape so that the landscape is more sustainable, using less water, fewer resources, and less energy to maintain it. Imagine a design that connects with the environment and enhances its uniqueness.

To begin a xeriscape, start with the design process because it requires that you gather information, ask questions about your needs and the site, and then integrate them with the site's capabilities. To do this, the *Xeriscape Handbook* becomes a guide to be used for formulating new designs, retrofitting old ones, or designing only segments of the landscape. Creating the xeriscape landscape need not be overwhelming. Do it slowly, in sections, and/or sequentially, and above all, enjoy the process.

Introduction

A landscape design is an attractively laid out plan, drawn to scale on paper, showing where things are in relationship to each other within a defined space. The plan shows how the space (the entire area being considered), the elements (all objects within the space), and the selected style (how the elements are organized) come together. The difference between a traditional landscape design and xeriscape is that xeriscape acknowledges water conservation and natural ecological processes as key players. Then, once the plan is implemented, its success will be determined by whether the design meets your needs, how suitable it is to the site, and local weather, soil, and environmental conditions, how plants perform and how much water, material (resources), and energy are required to maintain it.

A xeriscape design can be any style—formal, informal, natural—or a combination. Each style can be adapted and designed to conserve water.

Formal design suggests a control of nature through its orderly, balanced grouping of elements. The elements either complement each other or stand alone as a focal point or accent. Trees and shrubs may be incorporated to reflect

Figure 2.1—Formal landscape design.

the geometry of buildings, lines of streets, or to enhance architectural forms. Some aspects of formal style include straight paths to the front door with symmetrical plantings on each side or a hedge as a wall or background border *(Figure 2.1)*. To save water with formal designs, select plants carefully to fit the site and design, harvest water where possible (see Chapter VI), and use low pressure irrigation such as drip systems.

Informal styles, on the other hand, are less geometric, exhibiting less defined edges and forms. Lines tend to blur into each other and, in many cases, informality may be emphasized with curvilinear flowing beds and asymmetrical, irregular shapes *(Figure 2.2)*. Plants are grouped together in masses that blend into each other rather than each having their own place. Water conservation and natural ecological processes are easily integrated into informal designs, especially when the plans mimic natural plant communities.

A **natural** style of design constitutes a totally different approach. Although elements are selected for design features such as form, texture, balance, and color, plants and elements are grouped according to their natural association, compatibility, water needs, and their ability to fill a certain niche. This natural approach is often referred to as an "ecological landscape" because the landscape design and home can encompass the wilderness and blend in with the surrounding area. Natural plant associations and natural environments such as deserts, prairies, foothills, and forests drive the design. Natural design styles are governed by different standards of maintenance. Manicured lawns, sheared hedges, or specimen plants are not encouraged. Instead, recycling nutrients, natural composting, natural precipitation, native plants, restoration, and sustainability are the goals *(Figure 2.3)*.

Figure 2.2—Informal landscape design.

Figure 2.3—Naturalized landscape design.

Today in our various urban, suburban, and rural communities, no one style may suit the site and the individual, so styles are often combined. Whatever you choose, first imagine how the site looked before it was developed. This will help you understand the natural environment. Then observe the landscape as it is now. Lastly, view the outdoors as an extension of the indoors, al-lowing the interior to flow outside. This approach will make it easier to organize the outside space, its elements, and your needs so that the design takes on meaning and compatibility to your lifestyle as well as to the natural environment. Even at the early preplanning stage, watering, water conservation, maintenance, and conservation of resources should be foremost in your thoughts.

To begin the design process (noting all the above), follow the phases and steps listed below. These will sharpen your focus and help you define and identify your priorities. Since memories are short, take notes as you proceed. Remember, you can use this process whether you are designing a new landscape, retrofitting or reviving an old one, or concentrating only on a specific area—just concentrate on the steps you are interested in.

Phase I: Sensing the Site

Sensing the site entails getting to know what you want and need, what the site has to offer, and what you can do to make the site your own.

STEP 1. THE INDOOR/OUTDOOR RELATIONSHIP

With pencil and paper in hand, pull up a chair, sit down in front of your favorite window, and relax. Take several minutes to look outside. Ask yourself: (a) From this view, what do I want the landscape to provide for me, my family and guests? (Be sure to consider how other household members feel as well.) It may help if you look outside a window and imagine what you see is a large room or a series of rooms with walls (potentially trees, shrubs, or fence), floors (possibly ground cover, lawn, or concrete), and ceilings (the sky, tree canopies, arbors, and vines). Imagine each room with a purpose such as recreation, public access, or views, entertain-ment, gardening, and/or functions such as storage, privacy, or shading the indoors. (b) From this view, ask yourself: How do I want the site to look from indoors? Can I translate my interests, living style, and tastes from the inside to the outside? (c) How will this look in different seasons? (d) What effect does the outside area have on this indoor room? What are the sun and shade patterns for each season? (e) How comfortable is this room? How do I want to feel in this room? Will the outdoor landscape achieve my goals? (f) Repeat this process for each major window in your house. Write your thoughts down each time.

STEP 2. THE OUTDOOR/INDOOR RELATIONSHIP

With pencil and paper in hand, take a chair outdoors, find a comfortable place to sit near your property line and face the house. Relax and take several minutes to look around. Imagine the space as you did when you were inside; you are now looking at it from another perspective. Ask yourself: (a) From this view, what do I want the landscape to provide for me, my family, and my guests? Which area appeals to me most? (b) How will I feel in this space? Would I feel comfortable? (c) What are the sun and shade patterns? (d) How do I want the site to look now and in the other seasons? How will this landscape change with the seasons? (e) What was this area before it was developed—prairie, forest, shrub land, or desert? Are there any vestiges remaining? Can any portion of the naturalized area be salvaged or restored? (f) What is the soil like? Has it been compromised? (g) What design style fits both the site and my tastes? (Pay attention to the entire site and house.) (h) What architectural forms such as round, straight, triangular, and what materials such as wood, brick, or concrete can be repeated in the landscape for cohesion and harmony? (i) Evaluate some of the outdoor tasks that will be needed such as mowing, raking, watering, then ask yourself: What do I or other family members enjoy doing? Are there any distasteful chores that can be eliminated by reintroducing natural processes such as allowing leaf litter or grass clippings to remain? (j) Repeat this process as you walk around the house along the front, back, and side property lines. Write your thoughts down for each space and view.

STEP 3. EXTENDING THE OUTDOOR VIEWS

Take several minutes to survey your neighbors' sites and your neighborhood. Ask yourself: (a) From this view, does my site blend in with the neighborhood and or natural surroundings aesthetically and ecologically? (b) How do I feel about the site and the house in relation to each other and to the neighborhood? (c) What season is it? How will these same areas look at other times of the year, especially winter? (d) What will improve and unify my site with the neighborhood and environment?

STEP 4. LOOKING AT SOIL

Up to now you have been looking at the obvious. What we sometimes fail to notice, but is critical to a xeriscape landscape is what we don't see—the soil. In the natural environment, soil develops over long periods of time. But in an established landscape, altering soil characteristics is a different matter. Soil may change dramatically in relatively brief periods of time and may do so several times depending on how the land is used and who and how many people have worked it. Because of this, urban and suburban soils are difficult to evaluate. Furthermore, you as the homeowner will most likely have little information about its history. Yet, the success of your landscape, plant performance, and efficient use of water and other resources will basically depend on the soil and how you manage it. For this reason, you should take the time to learn about your soil. Before you start a design on paper, refer to Chapter III for several step-by-step exercises that will help you determine your soil's characteristics.

STEP 5. GATHERING IDEAS

This is the time to gather ideas and more clearly define what appeals to you. Thumb through books and magazines and take photographs of areas you find attractive. Look around and explore designs and gardens from other sources such as parks, neighboring landscapes, and natural areas. Ask yourself what do they have that you like and how might they fit into your plan. Natural landscapes are ideal for inspiration, especially with regard to saving water and nurturing ecological processes. For example: rock formations on a steep slope control soil erosion as well as collect moisture for plant roots; dry streams designed along drainage ditches take advantage of water runoff and can be used

Figure 2.4—Dry stream—an idea from nature.

for plants that need moisture; natural thickets of shrubs create shelters for wildlife as well as privacy screens; and prairies or meadows can substitute for lawns *(Figure 2.4)*.

STEP 6. TAKING A BREAK

Recess for several hours or days until you can review the site and your thoughts with fresh insight, then answer the following questions: How practical and realistic are your thoughts and ideas? Do your ideas incorporate saving water and do they nurture or maintain natural areas or ecological processes? Are you comfortable with your answers? If you are, you are ready for Phase II.

Phase II: Learning or Reviewing the Basics

Review your notes and then put them aside. Although you read Chapter I, you may want to review it. This is also a good time to jump ahead to Chapter III and do the exercises on soil. Begin focusing on ecological processes, sustainability, maintenance, xeriscape principles, irrigation, recycling, and composting. These terms can be found in the glossary. Do not skip any of the suggested readings, as you will be less prepared for the following steps. Once you have read and are comfortable with the terms and information, you may want to revise some of your ideas gathered in Phase I, Step 5. You are now ready to start Phase III: Initiating the Design on Paper.

Phase III: Initiating the Design on Paper

If you have completed all the steps in Phases I and II, you are ready to commit your plan to paper. You will need a plot plan and/or base plan (see Step 1), a clipboard and notebook or graph paper to write measurements on, tissue or tracing paper, and vellum or graph paper, pencils, eraser, ruler, something to draw angles and circles with such as a compass, template, triangle, or protractor, a 50- to 100-foot measuring tape, a roll of string, large nails or small stakes to secure the string into the ground, a hard, flat working surface, and masking tape to keep the paper stable on the surface.

STEP 1. DRAWING PLOT AND BASE PLANS

A plot plan is an official record that usually accompanies the title deed. It is generally drawn to scale showing the outline of the house, driveway, and property lines. The scale may be 1 inch equaling 20, 30, or 40 feet, depending on property size. If you have a plot plan, you should verify a few of the measurements as things may have changed since the initial survey. If you do not have the official recorded plot plan, you can contact your county public works or assessor's

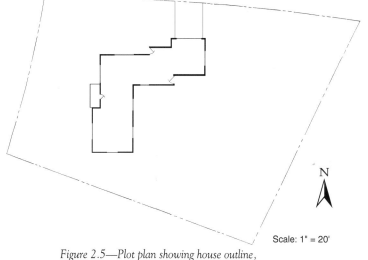

Scale: 1" = 20'

Figure 2.5—Plot plan showing house outline, property lines, and driveway.

EXAMPLE OF A BASE PLAN INVENTORY

House, buildings, and other structures (draw with a solid line):

- windows, doors, driveways, sidewalks, patios, and terraces
- water spigots and roof overhangs
- arrows showing views outside in and inside out
- fences, walls, telephone poles, and other structures

Property boundaries and easements (draw with a dashed line):

- electric, water, cable, utility, and gas lines
- sewage and water flow
- any shared walkways, driveways, or common areas

Direction of water flow (mark with arrows):

- water flow, waterways
- roof eaves and downspouts
- adjacent flow across property
- paved surfaces

Weather and microclimates (mark with arrows or shading):

- prevailing winds
- slope orientation
- sun and shady areas
- wet or dry spots

Existing features:

- topography such as slopes and hills
- natural features such as rock outcrops, creeks, and ponds
- existing features such as trees, shrubs, shrub masses, lawn, flower beds, and sculptures
- adjacent features and structures offsite that may influence your planning such as buildings, night lighting, and alleys

General information:

- owner and address
- north arrow
- scale of drawing

office. Or, you can draw one yourself on paper (as follows), use a computer drawing program, or you can hire a surveyor. The plot plan will serve as the basis of your design (*Figure 2.5*).

A base plan is the story of your site. It not only summarizes what is physically there, but it also lists conditions (such as easements) that will or do affect the site. It will guide you when implementing windbreaks, shading areas, avoiding interference with utility lines, and diverting water from roof lines. Using the base plan as a guide, you can create and draw your landscape design.

Draw the base plan using the plot plan for basic measurements, or you can hire a professional surveyor. Drawing your own base plan will help you get to know your property well. For information on easements (legal areas giving others limited use of or access to your property), planning and zoning restrictions, or other regulations that limit how you can use your land, contact your county, city, or neighborhood association.

A completed base plan should show the following items as they relate to each other. Step 2 will help you measure and define these items (*Figure 2.6*).

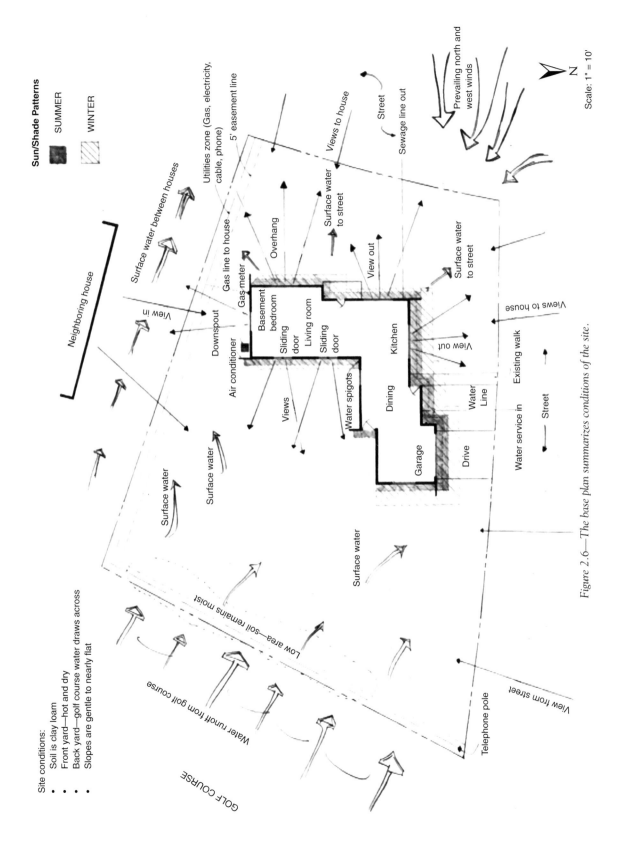

Sun/Shade Patterns

SUMMER

WINTER

Site conditions:
- Soil is clay loam
- Front yard—hot and dry
- Back yard—golf course water draws across
- Slopes are gentle to nearly flat

GOLF COURSE

Water runoff from golf course

Low area—soil remains moist

Surface water

Telephone pole

View from street

Water service in   Existing walk

Street

Views to house

Water Line

Drive

Garage

Dining

Kitchen

View out

Surface water to street

View out

Living room

Sliding door

Sliding door

Basement bedroom

Overhang

Gas meter

Gas line to house

Utilities zone (Gas, electricity, cable, phone)

5' easement line

Surface water to street

Views

Water spigots

Surface water

Surface water

Surface water between houses

Neighboring house

View in

Downspout

Air conditioner

Street

Sewage line out

Views to house

Prevailing north and west winds

N

Scale: 1" = 10'

Figure 2.6—The base plan summarizes conditions of the site.

STEP 2. MEASURING THE SITE FOR THE BASE PLAN

DEFINING THE SCALE

You can consolidate all the information on a plot plan on your base plan. Then, select a scale to work in. Depending on the property's size, 1 inch = 10 feet or 1 inch = 8 feet are easiest. For large properties, you may need to work in a scale of 1 inch = 20 feet. For greater detail, it can be drawn at $1/4$-inch =1 foot. You may already have a plot plan from a surveyor at a smaller scale. If you do, transpose it to the new scale. You can also enlarge the plot plan on a copier. Before you do, draw a 1-inch line on the plan, copy the plan in the enlarge mode, and then check the previously drawn line to make sure the enlargement is accurate. If you are drawing your own plan and need to know which paper size will accomodate it, draw an outline of the entire property at the new scale and add a few inches. Easy paper sizes to work with are 11 x 17 or 24 x 36-inch sheets.

MEASURING THE SITE

If you do not already have a plot plan, the first thing you'll need to do is establish some baselines to determine site boundaries and the house location. This will make it easier to position elements in your landscape design. With your clipboard and paper, go to one corner of the house. Take a tape measure and extend the side of the house to the property line or boundary. Mark it with a string and measure the line, then draw it on the paper noting its length. This becomes the baseline. Continue to measure and record all sides and their distances from corners to property lines. Measure all sides of the house (noting angles when they are not right angles) and add the house and its dimensions on the plan. Use the baseline to measure other structures such as trees, posts, etc. in the landscape. Note all measurements on paper (*Figure 2.7*).

If the boundary lines are straight, but not parallel, you will need two baselines to measure the boundaries accurately. Go to a corner of the house. With the tape measure, extend the straight line of the wall until you reach the property line. This is baseline #1. Mark it with a string and measure its length. Go back to the same corner and at a 90-degree angle to baseline #1 extend a second line to the boundary and measure its length. This is baseline #2. Measure the distance from your baselines to the boundaries at two more points to set the boundary lines (*Figure 2.8*).

If the boundary lines are not straight, divide each baseline into 10-foot increments. Using a 90-degree angle at each increment, measure the distance between the baseline and the boundary. After marking several points along the boundary, you will be able to draw the property line. Note your measurements on paper.

After completing your measurements, your plan should show property lines, the outside dimensions of your house, driveway, and walkways, and where your house sits on the property. At the appropriate scale, draw the plan on vellum or reproducible paper using solid lines for buildings and dashed lines for boundaries (*Figure 2.9*).

ADDING ELEMENTS TO THE BASE PLAN (SEE BASE PLAN INVENTORY IN STEP 1)

To measure other elements in the landscape, use the baselines. When drawing the plan to scale, use faint, dotted lines for elements that will be changed and use arrows for compass direction showing aspect, winds, views, and water flow. Outside the property margins, note the date, scale, and north arrow (*Figure 2.10*).

MEASURING ELEVATIONS

In some cases, the site may exhibit obvious changes in elevation. If they are small, you can make notes on the plan. If they are large, such as a steep slope or drop in grade, you may want to measure them for a more accurate reading, especially if the changes in elevation affect soil erosion, water run-off, and sun and shade patterns.

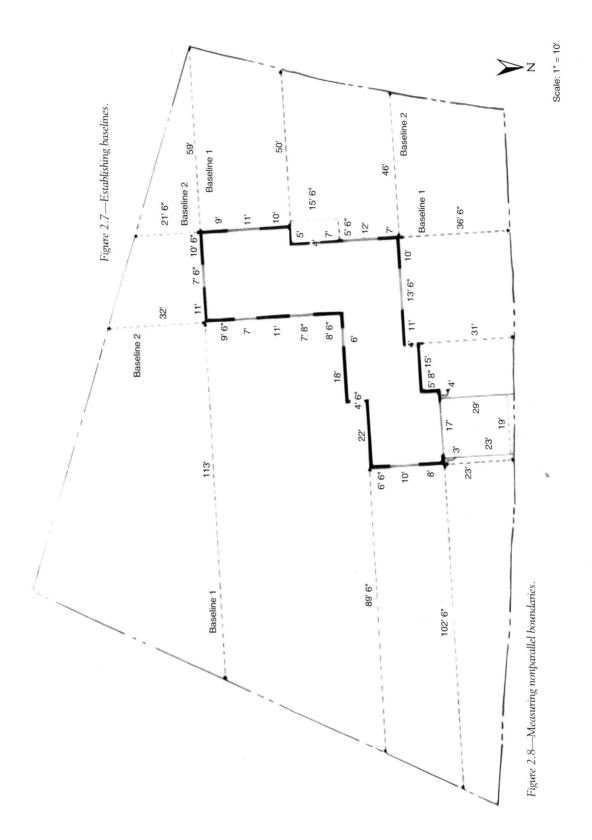

Figure 2.7—Establishing baselines.

Figure 2.8—Measuring nonparallel boundaries.

Scale: 1" = 10'

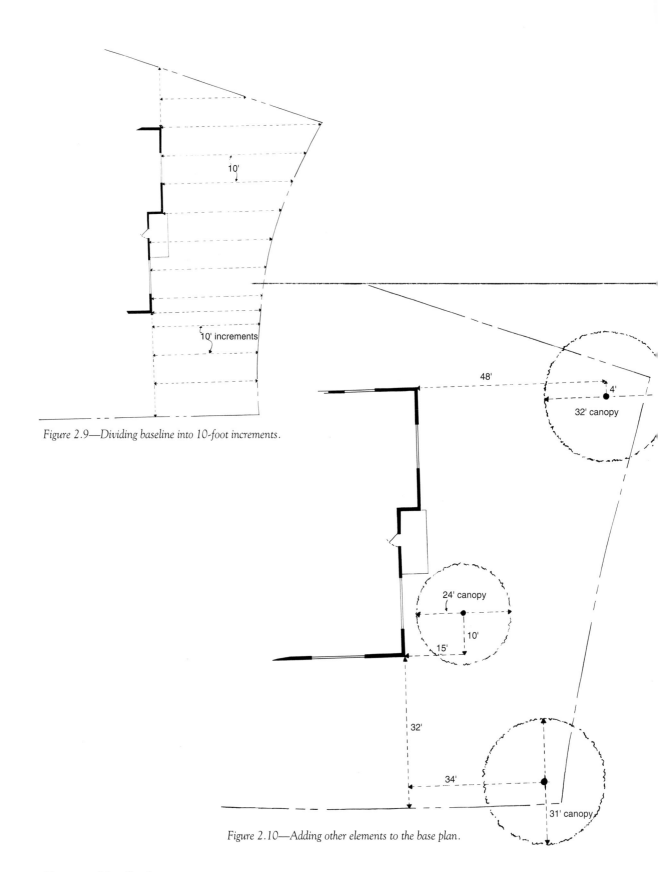

10'

10' increments

Figure 2.9—Dividing baseline into 10-foot increments.

48'

4'

32' canopy

24' canopy

10'

15'

32'

34'

31' canopy

Figure 2.10—Adding other elements to the base plan.

The angle of a slope can be expressed either as a gradient or as a percentage. The gradient (G) is shown as a ratio between the vertical distance or height (V) and horizontal distance or length (H): G = V:H. A slope that rises 5 feet in elevation in 10 horizontal feet has a ratio of 5:10 or 1:2; a slope that rises 10 feet in 100 horizontal feet has a ratio of 10 to 100 or 1:10. These ratios can also be expressed as percentages. The slope with a 1:2 ratio is $^1/_2$ or a 50 percent slope; a 10:100 ratio is equivalent to $^1/_{10}$ or a 10 percent slope (*Figure 2.11*).

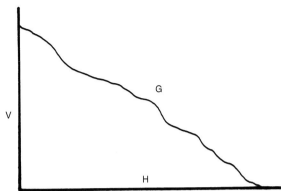

Figure 2.11—Diagram of slope gradient.

TABLE 2.1

Percentage	Ratio	Comment	Illustration
100 percent	1:1	very steep	
50 percent	1:2	highly subject to soil erosion	
33 percent	1:3	maximum slope for lawn subject to runoff	
25 percent	1:4	maximum slope for safe mowing	
20 percent	1:5	comfortable for ramps	
10 percent or less	1:10	gentle slope	

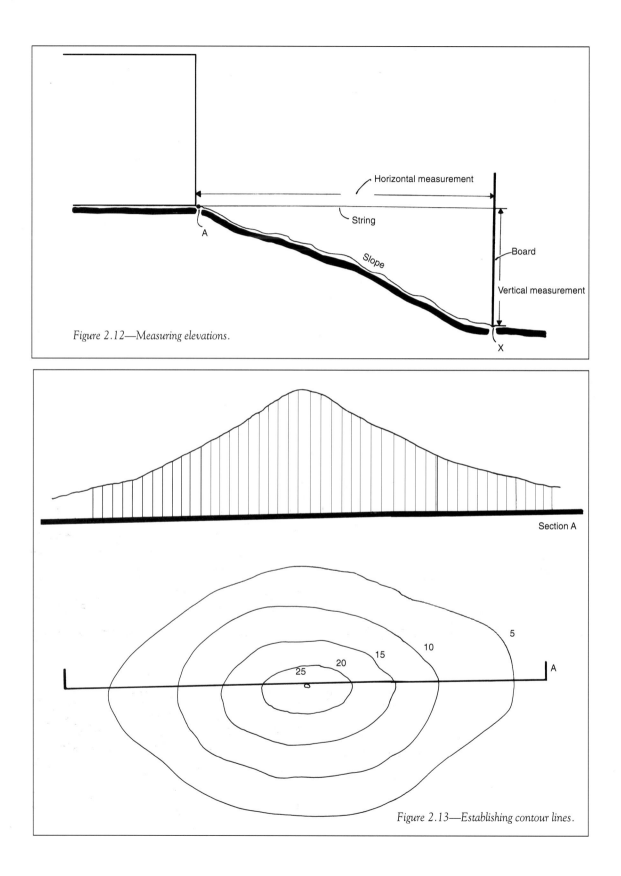

Figure 2.12—Measuring elevations.

Horizontal measurement

String

A

Slope

Board

Vertical measurement

X

Section A

5

10

15

20

25

A

Figure 2.13—Establishing contour lines.

There are several ways to measure the elevation of a slope, but for small areas, the following procedure is sufficient. It involves extending a level line from one point of the property to another and then taking measurements from that level line to the ground. You will need a string, a carpenter's level, a 6- to 10-foot board, and a measuring tape. The level line can be determined with the string and level. First, designate the lowest point on the property you are measuring as point X. Place the board upright at this point and stabilize it. You will use this point X to measure all other elevations. Second, stand at the high point (A) of the slope and secure the string in the ground. Take the string from point A to point X, using the level to verify that the string remains level. Secure the string to the board. For the vertical distance, measure the height of the board where the string meets it. Then, measure the length of the string for the horizontal distance *(Figure 2.12)*.

Select other points along the slope or on the property that you want to measure. Walk to each point and read the elevation and record it on your base plan. By plotting points of equal elevation, you can form contour lines. For larger, more uneven terrain, you can use the same principle, but use a transit and a measuring stick. With large, complicated sites, you may need surveying equipment or you may want to hire a professional surveyor *(Figure 2.13)*.

CREATING A PHOTOGRAPHIC PERSPECTIVE

In addition to drawing the base plan, it is helpful to photograph the site and its surroundings from different viewpoints within and outside of the property as well as from your house. These photos give a different perspective and will remind you of elements you may otherwise ignore or forget. They also serve as "before" memories. Individual 3x5-inch photographs highlight specific areas such as views from the inside, outside cables, wiring, and things we see, yet overlook every day. By overlapping and mounting the photographs

Figure 2.14—Create a photographic perspective.

on a tagboard, you can create a panorama that gives a broader view of the site and surrounding settings. These can also help you visualize some of your ideas by drawing them on tracing paper and placing them over the prints (*Figure 2.14*).

Phase IV: Composing the Conceptual Design

Now that you have evaluated your site and mapped it out on paper, you are ready to transform your ideas into useful space. This is not your final composition, but a conceptual design.

STEP 1. REVIEWING IDEAS

Before you put pencil to paper, refresh your memory by reviewing your notes, ideas collected from magazines and photographs, your needs and aspirations, as well as your philosophy on watering and conserving resources. Once you are satisfied with the above, prioritize them on a list.

STEP 2. DEFINING ACTIVITIES

Take your base plan and overlay it with tissue paper. With the photographs (if you took them) at your side for reference, on the tissue freely outline areas showing how they will be used and the approximate space needed for that purpose. General activity areas may include public and private spaces, recreation, entertainment, and service areas. Try to group activities that overlap or use the same space. For example, a space for badminton and a children's play area may actually be one and the same, or a place to read and entertain guests may share similar borders. Experiment with different ideas to see how they will work and draw several plans before settling on one. You can validate your choices by going back outside and visualizing the activities and spaces. Keep in mind that flat areas are easier to define on paper but areas of relief may dictate different uses than what you envisioned. If sizes or locations are inappropriate, correct them now (*Figure 2.15*).

STEP 3. EVALUATING MICROCLIMATES AND SOIL CAPABILITIES

Microclimates and soil (see Chapter III) are key to developing ecologically sound and sensitive xeriscape landscapes. In natural ecosystems, plants arrange themselves according to microclimates and soil conditions. The microclimates on your site may be warmer, cooler, windier, wetter, or drier than the norm. They vary because of differences in sun and shade as well as wind patterns, topography, soil, plants, structures, and other materials. Even the smallest microclimate, such as behind a rock or hedge, should be taken into consideration for appropriate plant placement.

The most significant microclimates on your site are created by sun and shade patterns which in turn affect temperature, soil moisture, and plant growth, as well as your own physical comfort. The more directly and longer the sun strikes an area, the warmer the area becomes and the greater the variance between sun and shade. A shaded area may be 10–15°F cooler, more humid, or darker than the area in the sun. At high elevations, microclimates are even more pronounced. Sunny areas feel very warm, while shady areas are quite cool.

Getting to know your microclimates is important. There is no substitute for spending time in the landscape at different times of the day and season to understand sun, shade, and wind patterns, and the extent of shadows and their density. Look at all the objects that cast shadows, pay attention to wind, watch plant responses to morning and afternoon sun, and note how heavy precipitation and times of drought affect your site (*Figure 2.16*).

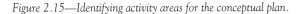

Figure 2.15—Identifying activity areas for the conceptual plan.

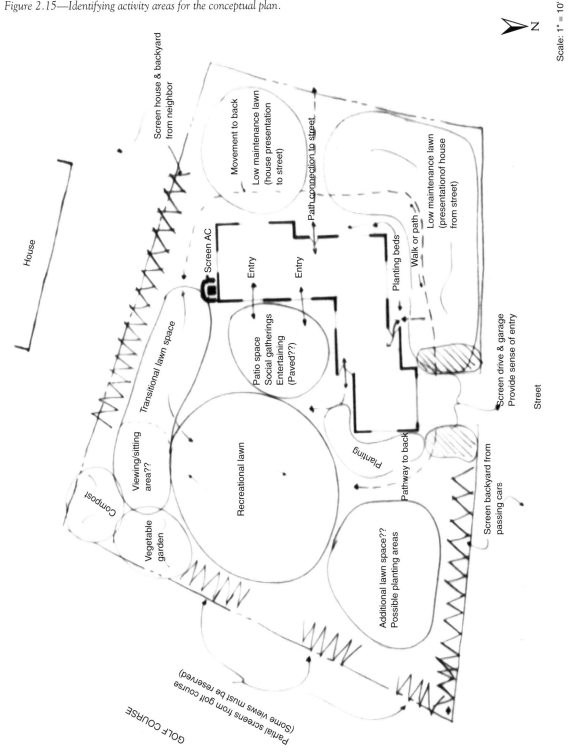

Scale: 1" = 10'

N

House

Screen house & backyard from neighbor

Movement to back

Low maintenance lawn (house presentation to street)

Path connection to street

Low maintenance lawn (presentationof house from street)

Screen AC

Entry

Entry

Planting beds

Walk or path

Transitional lawn space

Patio space
Social gatherings
Entertaining
(Paved??)

Viewing/sitting area??

Compost

Vegetable garden

Recreational lawn

Planting

Pathway to back

Screen drive & garage
Provide sense of entry

Street

Screen backyard from passing cars

Additional lawn space??
Possible planting areas

Partial screens from golf course
(Some views must be reserved)

GOLF COURSE

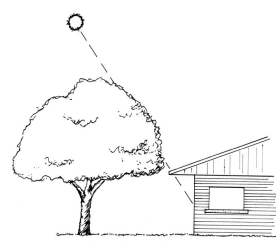

Figure 2.16—Understand sun and shade patterns.

Once you have familiarized yourself with the microclimates, make a copy of the completed base plan or use a tissue overlay. With a few crayons, summarize microclimates and soil conditions with colors. Color shady areas gray, sunny areas yellow, windy spots black, wet spots blue, and dry areas brown. This activity will help you assign activities and plants appropriately, in the appropriate microclimate with the corresponding soil conditions. For example, did you inadvertently place your vegetable garden in the shade or a tree in a wet area? (*Figure 2.17*).

The basic microclimates on your site should encompass the four major exposures: south, north, east, and west.

SOUTHERN EXPOSURE

House walls, slopes, hedges, and other structures that face south are exposed to more sunlight than those facing north. These areas are warmer, encouraging increased soil evaporation, faster plant transpiration, earlier snow melt, and drier soil. Southern exposure usually means a longer growing season into fall and an earlier warm-up in spring. You may find that spring bulbs bloom several weeks earlier on the south side than on the north. Early warm-up can be a concern because plants are still in danger of being killed by frosts. On the other hand, a southern exposure is excellent for a driveway or major walkway because snow melts rapidly. It is also an ideal orientation for an outdoor winter room, particularly at high elevations. Summer shade can be provided

by an overhang planted with vines or a large deciduous tree with a high canopy. Areas that are not shaded can be planted with species that naturally grow in full sun. Many of these plants are from cold deserts, semiarid shrub lands, or short- and mid-grass prairies (*Figure 2.18*).

NORTHERN EXPOSURE

Unlike the south side, northern exposures may experience shade year-round. These areas are the last to warm up in spring and the first to cool down in fall. The relative difference between north and south orientation is greatest in winter. Depending on latitude and the size of the structure blocking the sun, long winter shadows can form, even from features off site. Less solar radiation also means less extreme temperature swings. The freezing and thawing of soil may not be an issue, but persistent snow cover might be. This is a maintenance problem if drive and walkways are located here. Plants that prefer cool, moist, shaded areas (such as those usually found in a forest's understory) and broadleaf evergreens are practical choices for a northern exposure. Plants that are marginally hardy in your zone may sometimes do better on the north side because they are not as exposed to the temperature fluctuations occurring in other parts of the landscape. The north side can also provide a cool, outdoor living area in summer (*Figure 2.19*).

EASTERN EXPOSURE

Areas exposed to the east are more protected from winter winds, and temperatures are more

Figure 2.17—Coloring the microclimates.

Scale: ³/₄" = 10'

N

Sunny

Moist

Dry & Hot

Shade

Figure 2.18—Southern exposure with plants such as juniper, sedums, and yuccas that grow in full sun.

Figure 2.20—Eastern exposure with plants from humid environments.

Figure 2.19—Northern exposure with ferns and broadleaf evergreen plants.

moderate than those with south or west orientations. They receive morning sunshine throughout the year, but at a relatively lower angle. In winter a minimal amount of heat accumulates, but in summer as noon approaches, the days can get quite warm. Eastern exposures in arid regions are preferred sites in summer for plants that are native to sunny, humid areas, either from higher elevations or from cooler climates. Here plants and people find relief in the afternoon shade. Large ornamental shrubs or small trees with low branches and moderate to delicate texture (lilacs, viburnums, hawthorns, crabapples, serviceberry, and mountain ash) can be positioned to filter the summer sun (*Figure 2.20*).

WESTERN EXPOSURE

Western exposures with morning shade and afternoon sun receive the sun at a low angle, but in summer, the afternoons can get very hot. On the west side, soils tend to suffer greater temperature swings and more rapid drying than those on the east. Late fall to early spring, warm sunny afternoons followed by cold nights can damage plant tissues, presented as cracks in young tree bark or a blackening of newly formed leaves and stems. Northwesterly cold winds intensify the damage. These winds can be modified. High speed and drying winds can be thwarted by dense plantings on the windward side of the site. Glare from snow or other light surfaces can also pose a problem. Locating small, upright evergreens on the west and northwest side near the house will serve to reduce glare.

Western exposure areas are comfortable on summer mornings, but afternoons should be shaded with a tall deciduous tree planted at a reasonable distance from the house. Plants that prefer dry soil and warm temperatures should also be planted here. Caused by unequal lighting of an eastern exposure, species that naturally grow in full sun (native to warm or high deserts) tend to lean toward the west. These should be planted in full exposure away from the shade of any structure (*Figure 2.21*).

Remember that the effects of sun and shade apply not only to main structures on the site,

Figure 2.21—Western exposure with uneven light may cause some plants to bend to one direction.

but also to less imposing structures such as fences, rocks, and walls.

TOPOGRAPHY

Topographic features also create microclimates. Unless relief is man-made, at the top and along slopes, the soil is generally rockier and more coarse; it drains well, but holds less moisture though it may receive more precipitation than at the base. The steeper the slope, the drier the soil. At the base, soil is finer, higher in nutrients, and retains more moisture. However, although the area may be moist, with low relative humidity and rapid evaporation, the low relative humidity can dry it out within a few days.

STEP 4. CONNECTING ACTIVITIES

Once spaces, microclimates, and activities are defined, the spaces need to be connected in order to make them accessible to you and others. Accessibility and circulation affect how people

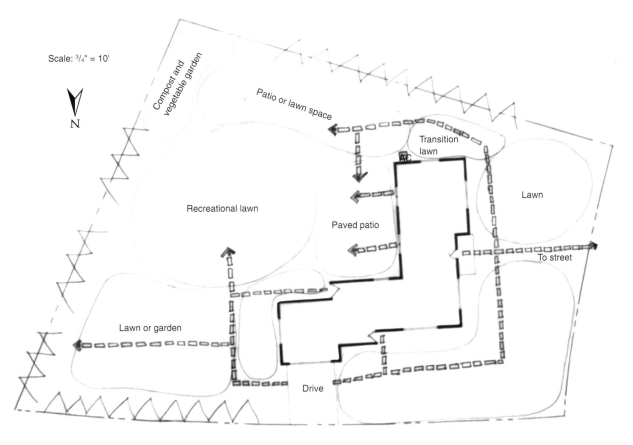

Scale: $^3/_4$" = 10'

N

Compost and vegetable garden

Patio or lawn space

Transition lawn

A/C

Lawn

Recreational lawn

Paved patio

Lawn or garden

To street

Drive

Figure 2.22—Circulation patterns show movement and accessibility.

move through and experience a landscape. You can sketch circulation patterns with arrows and lines between the spaces to show accessibility and movement to and from each activity and the house (Figure 2.22). These will represent the way you and others will move in and around the landscape. These routes should be simple and safe. Areas and paths intended for direct access should measure 4 to 5 feet wide and be clearly lit with the end in view. This is especially true for public or main entrances. It may be necessary to provide landing platforms and parking for visitors. These should be considered in this phase of the design.

Leisurely paths connecting gardens and areas of enjoyment can be less direct and meandering with points of interest along the way. The width of these areas is often dictated by the surrounding vegetation. Avoid lining the path with vigorous shrubs or ground covers that may quickly encroach on the walking surface and that demand frequent pruning and maintenance (Figure 2.23).

Service paths include those that get you to and from the work areas. These should be 2 to 3 feet wide, or what is most comfortable for you and the materials/supplies you may need

Figure 2.23—An overgrown path requires frequent maintenance.

to haul back and forth. Border plants along the path should be set back far enough so they do not interfere with safety and ease of movement, or get crushed and damaged by equipment (Figure 2.24).

Other circulation areas include decks and patios as they connect the indoors to the outside. A standard measurement for patios is 125 square feet per person; however, the size of an outdoor space is more accurately defined by its use, circulation patterns, furniture, and, simply, "what feels right."

Figure 2.24—Service paths should be wide enough to accommodate equipment.

As space, accessibility, and circulation are considered, the character of the landscape begins to emerge. This is a good time to experiment with different styles and the seasonal aspects of the design. Formal styles tend to be more constant throughout the year; whereas, informal and natural styles are variable. Try to visualize the site in all seasons, especially in winter when structure and style are so obviously dominant (*Figure 2.25*).

Figure 2.25—Structure and design style are more obvious in winter than in summer.

STEP 5. REFINING THE SPACE

Once you are comfortable with the spaces, activities assigned to them, and the movement among them, think again (as you did at the beginning of the design process) of each area as a room. The ceiling (sky) and floor (ground) may already exist, but can be modified by materials and other structures. For example, what may be bare soil can become lawn, other vegetation cover, or flagstone. The walls may already exist (neighboring fences, houses, trees) or they can be created. In many instances, where they are placed and what materials are used for walls (vertical elements) should be influenced by the site and your needs. For example, if the site is windy, you might deflect the wind with a wall of evergreen trees, or if you want privacy, the walls may consist of a fence. You might want to sketch out specific rooms on a tissue overlay (*Figure 2.26*).

STEP 6. BUILDING IN CONSERVATION, IRRIGATION, AND ECOLOGICAL CONSIDERATIONS

Irrigation has enabled us to grow plants from many different climates and, in many cases, has directed our landscape designs to depend on it.

This is the time to evaluate your plans for water use and irrigation requirements. Do your ideas encourage water conservation and efficient use

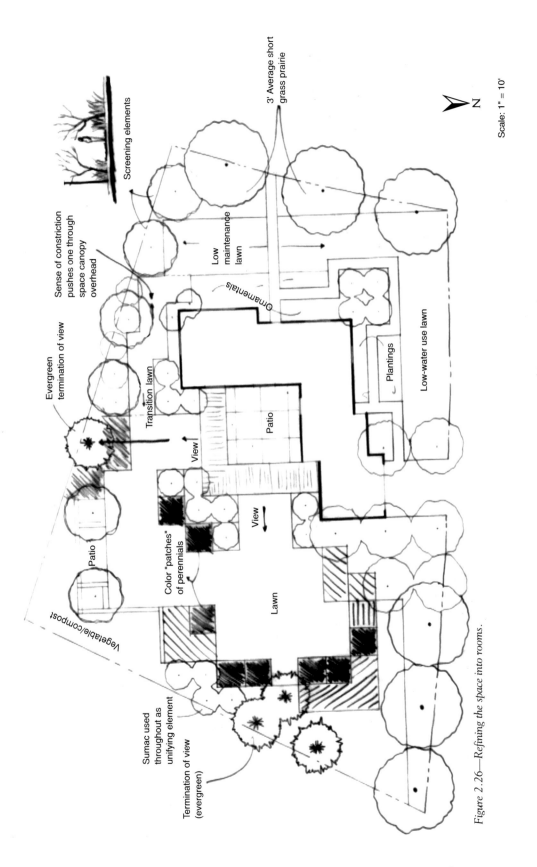

Screening elements

3' Average short grass prairie

Scale: 1" = 10'

N

Sense of constriction pushes one through space canopy overhead

Low maintenance lawn

Ornamentals

Evergreen termination of view

Transition lawn

Plantings

Low-water use lawn

Patio

View

Patio

Color "patches" of perennials

Vegetable/compost

View

Lawn

Sumac used throughout as unifying element

Termination of view (evergreen)

Figure 2.26—Refining the space into rooms.

of resources? Is the design sensitive to ecological processes that will minimize the use of water and other resources? Have you considered if and how you will water? Are you applying xeriscape principles? How have you built conservation and efficiency into your plan? This would be a good time to read through Chapters IV, V, and VI for more information on conservation techniques and irrigation. Use the following lists for ideas:

WATER CONSERVATION DESIGN TIPS

- Cool-season turf grass is a major water user. Convert some areas of lawn into decking, porous paving, or mulch, or select a warm-season lawn.
- Do not put in a cool-season lawn on berms or steep slopes because water runs off too quickly without penetrating the soil. Control erosion and runoff on slopes with low-water–use vegetation, and consider terraces or contours.
- Keep areas of high water needs to a minimum. Cool-season lawns in arid or semiarid areas should be installed only when something else won't do. If large areas of lawn are necessary, select a grass that requires less water and prepare the soil 6 to 8 inches deep (see Lawns, pages 53–56).
- Do not cultivate lawns in shady areas or those with problem soil.
- Design and group plants with similar soil, exposure, and water needs. Match the plants with their appropriate microclimates. Use these microclimates, along with the shelter that buildings and structures provide to your advantage.
- Eliminate plants that need irrigation from areas that are neither seen nor used. Use side yards as part of the back or front so that they are more functional.
- Keep beds to a manageable size. Avoid odd-shaped planting beds that are difficult to water with overhead sprinkler systems.

- Where appropriate, modify conditions to reduce water loss. For example, afternoon shade and windbreaks reduce transpiration. Incorporate in your design protection from drying winds and intense sun; shade areas to reduce transpiration.
- Do not use plants with high water requirements under large trees with dense canopies or under trees with shallow roots because the resultant competition for water will necessitate more water.
- Locate dryland plants where the microclimates are hot and dry and where irrigation is unreliable. Examples include uplands, steep slopes, and windy sites, where soils are shallow, coarse, and fast draining with little water retention. Situate plants that need moisture in flat areas with fine-textured soil or in areas that retain moisture.
- Use mulch to reduce soil evaporation in the bare spaces between plants. Mulch also protects the soil from erosion and crusting.
- Plan for the appropriate use of plants in dry areas that become saturated in upper layers after rains, but dry quickly from high evaporation and high temperatures.

IRRIGATION CONSIDERATIONS

Irrigation is a way of artificially supplying water to plants by means of basins, troughs, pipes, and hoses. Although it enables us to grow plants from all over the world, it is difficult to replace the uniformity of distribution and simplicity that natural precipitation provides. Preventing waste from runoff, applying just the right amount of water, and meeting plants' needs are all learned skills. For any mechanical irrigation system, its success is determined by the irrigation design, installation, operator, and maintenance. To help ensure an efficient irrigation system, your landscape should be designed and organized with irrigation in mind.

- Evaluate how often during the growing season you will need to provide supplemental water.
- Know your water source.
- Determine how much money you are willing to spend on water.
- Identify which plants will need the most water during the summer, and which will need watering in winter. Select and group plants according to their water needs and intended irrigation methods. Avoid combining plants with different cultural requirements.
- Tailor watering to the plant's needs, site, exposure, and season.
- Go through your plan to see if it can be modified to render watering or irrigation systems more efficient.
- Be aware of the limitations of irrigation (see Chapter VI on irrigation).

IRRIGATION DESIGN TIPS

- Eliminate planting in areas that are difficult to water such as tapering or odd-shaped planting beds, slopes, and narrow strips (*Figure 2.27*).
- Eliminate planting in areas where plants receive too much water from one direction or are located under overhangs.

Figure 2.27—A difficult area to water and maintain.

- Eliminate or limit cultivating areas where reflected heat and light enhance evaporation.
- Modify irrigation methods for slopes, low spots, and other areas where water behaves differently than on flat surfaces.
- Eliminate irrigation overflow onto paved areas and sidewalks by using drip or bubbler systems.
- Coordinate systems so that one area uses the runoff from another.
- Isolate turf grass watering from other plantings.
- Organize irrigation types and times according to sun, wind, elevation, and soil characteristics.
- Determine water zones for high, moderate, low, and very low water needs such as:
  High irrigation zones: $1^1/_2$ inches per week—Kentucky bluegrass and trees from lower ground in moist deciduous forests such as maple, birch, and willow.
  Moderate irrigation zones: $^3/_4$ inch per week—plants from transitional zones between prairies and forests such as honey locust and burr oak.
  Low irrigation zones: 1 inch every few weeks—plants from short- and mid-grass prairies such as sumac, mountain mahogany, and Gambel oak.
  Seldom irrigated zones: desert shrubs such as fernbush and Apache plume.
- Use drip and bubbler emitters for nonturf areas where appropriate.
- If water drains quickly (more than 1 inch per hour), use a drip system or cultivate plants adapted to dry soil. If water is draining slowly ($^1/_4$ inch per hour), it may run off the surface before it's absorbed. In this case, plan for watering in repetitive cycles.
- Plan some irrigation using harvested water or gray water (see following list).

WATER HARVESTING AND GRAY WATER (*see Chapter VI*)

- Situate plants in areas where you can make use of the runoff from adjacent areas.
- Know your soil in order to design and plan for water storage.
- Plan to collect and use rainwater off roofs, downspouts, and hard surfaces.
- Redirect runoff and collect water for future use either in the soil or in containers.
- Choose surface materials that retain soil moisture and prevent water runoff.
- Design small, depressed islands of plantings in and among hard surfaces to make use of runoff and to cool the soil underneath.
- Develop a plan for using snowmelt.
- Recycle water from the rinse cycles of your dishwasher and washing machine.

ECOLOGICAL CONSIDERATIONS IN DESIGN

Integrating ecological processes is easy using a natural style of design, but these processes can be incorporated in other styles as well. Site design that takes these processes into consideration, whatever the style, requires an understanding of natural systems and how our activities affect them.

Figure 2.28—Natural thickets of hawthorn or Gambel oak are good substitutes for hedges and borders.

- Select, choose, and group plants that naturally grow together. Match them according to their growing requirements, water needs, and site preferences.
- Favor plant species native to your area.
- Avoid disrupting soil structure and soil organisms by minimizing or eliminating soil disturbance.
- Allow plant debris to remain as mulch; leave grass clippings to recycle nutrients (see Chapter IV on mulch).
- Use compost for soil amendments and mulch for bedding plants, flower beds, and container plantings.

Figure 2.29—For a more arid climate, use golden currant (left) instead of forsythia (right).

- Use hedgerows (combinations of different plants in rows) instead of hedges (same plants grown in a row), prairies instead of lawn, thickets instead of planting borders, and tree groves or groups instead of single specimens (*Figure 2.28*).
- Group plants of varying root depths with noncompeting water needs, such as bulbs planted 6 to 8 inches deep growing with fibrous rooted plants that use only the top 4 to 6 inches.
- Group plants with sequential dormancy and growth cycles so one is dormant while another is active.
- In arid and semiarid areas, where possible, use shrubs in place of trees as the dominant plant type. Many shrubs grow in transitional areas between humid and arid regions or on dry sides of prairies and forests. These environments provide a greater number of plants adaptable to drier environments than trees. For every land-

Figure 2.30—Plant group based on natural associations— piñon pine, yucca, and sage.

scape use and microclimate you have, there is most likely an appropriate shrub (*Figure 2.29*).
- Design plant groups based on their natural communities or associations (*Figure 2.30*).
- Be realistic about the maintenance you are willing to provide or perform in the future and plan accordingly.

STEP 7. ELEMENTS IN DESIGN

The more you work the design through, the easier it is to clarify and hone your ideas. When you reach this stage, you begin to move from the functional aspects of your plan to the aesthetic ones. This is where you focus on detail and plan for combinations of elements based on their design characteristics such as size, texture, color, and form.

Before purchasing specific materials or plants, evaluate your prospective choices for what you want them to do, and envision their size, shape, and form from youth to maturity. For some ideas, look around your local area. Some of the most stable and valued properties are those with mature landscapes where trees and shrubs are thriving. There are probably trees fifty to one hundred years or more old that have performed well for several generations. Ideally, every tree, shrub, flower, and lawn should be planted only after considering its overall effect from its beginning to its maturity.

As you begin to select and introduce the plants from your plan, situate them where they can develop without interference from the house or other obstacles. For example, large shade trees should be planted at least 20 feet away from the house to avoid branch damage in the event of a storm. Trees such as silver maple that break easily should be planted even farther away. Avoid overhead and underground utility lines. Large trees under and near overhead utilities can pose a danger as they grow, and will ultimately require some pruning. This may result in an unnatural appearance, potentially a shorter life span for the tree, and unnecessary expenditures. Equally important are underground lines. Tree roots and underground utility lines often coexist without problems; however, roots may invade

Figure 2.31—Plants as structural tools can enhance vertical lines.

Figure 2.32—Plants can be used to modify winds.

cracked plumbing. Trees such as poplar and willow have aggressive roots that can enter cracks in water lines. Plant these species at least 80 to 100 feet from any known water source. The greatest potential for damage to underground lines occurs while planting. Before siting or digging, locate your underground utilities by contacting your utility provider.

When selecting other materials, keep in mind the overall ambience they contribute to the landscape. For example, brick and wood appear earthy, imparting warmth and friendliness. Stone, asphalt, and concrete are harsher, conveying a colder, more aloof atmosphere.

While placing the different materials and plants in your plan, ask yourself four questions: (a) What function is it meant to serve and will it succeed in doing so? (b) What structure should it provide or fulfill and does it? (c) What are the environmental controls and influences? (d) What are the aesthetic characteristics? Your responses to these questions will help you fine-tune your selections or find alternatives, if necessary, for your final choices.

PLANT FUNCTIONS

Plants perform several functions in the landscape, such as architectural components, engineering elements, and climate or environmental control. They may serve one or all three of these purposes.

Plant structure

Plants as structural tools create rooms and define space. You can use trees and shrubs for walls, screens, or barriers. Ground covers can be used for paths and floors. Structurally, plants can enhance the vertical and horizontal lines of buildings, frame boundaries, divide areas, control traffic, and provide background (*Figure 2.31*).

Plants and environmental controls

As environmental controls, plants modify climate by tempering winds, buffering or modifying temperatures, filtering dust, creating shade, and intercepting precipitation. If placed strategically, they can minimize glare, reduce noise and air pollution, and curb wind, soil, and water erosion (*Figure 2.32*).

Plants' aesthetic features

Aesthetically, most plants are viewed in terms of the beauty and comfort they bring to the landscape. They provide visual accent and background, textural interest, color, and seasonal variation. Many of these qualities are derived from plant textures. Plant textures comprise thickness, size, color and shape of foliage and stems, and surface finish, as well as the size and flexibility of their branches. Coarse plants have stout, rigid stems, few branches, and large foliage. These plants are best used as accents, in the background or in large areas, and should be limited in number. Medium-textured plants are by far the most dominant in availability and should dominate in quantity as well. They are effective in groups and provide a backdrop or transition between coarse- and fine-textured elements. Fine-textured plants appear feathery, light, airy, or lacy. They boast small foliage, delicate stems, and many fine branchlets. Used en masse, they provide a neutral background in group plantings *(Figure 2.33)*. Plants' winter textures are also worth consideration and can be quite different from those of summer. Walnut, Kentucky coffee tree, and goldenrain tree display a fine summer texture and a coarse winter texture.

Colors also manifest textural qualities. Dark colors are coarse and bold; paler colors are airy and light. The various shades of leaves and flowers can create drama in a landscape design especially one built around a monochromatic (one color) scheme. It is difficult to envision the many shades of one color until you plan a monochromatic garden.

VISUAL RELATIONSHIPS IN DESIGN

As you make specific selections, concentrate on evaluating the visual relationships among the elements. Note the effect a single element and combinations of elements have on the overall design. How will the selected trees look with the ground cover? Do the stone paths complement the style or materials of the house? Some basic principles of relationships among elements to think about include unity, harmony, continuity, repetition, accent, balance, scale, proportion, simplicity, and variety.

Unity

Unity effects harmony among the elements. It is the matrix that ties all the pieces together, bringing isolated groups into the fold as part of a whole. Unity can be achieved either by keeping with a continuous theme or by repeating

Figure 2.33—Plants with fine texture can appear feathery and light.

elements. For example, a ground cover can unify the landscape, and several groups of shrubs repeated throughout the landscape can also create a oneness that pulls otherwise unlike elements together *(Figure 2.34)*.

Accent

Accent draws attention to an element. Different shapes, forms, sizes, colors, and textures can provide an emphasis depending on where they are placed *(Figure 2.35)*.

Balance

Balance is an asymmetrical or symmetrical visual equilibrium in a composition. It can be achieved by the scale (the size of elements in

Figure 2.34—Groundcovers unify elements in the landscape.

Figure 2.35—Shapes and forms can provide an accent or focal point.

Figure 2.36—Balance achieved with size and proportion.

relation to other elements) and the proportion or dimensional relationships among the elements (*Figure 2.36*).

Simplicity and variety

When designing the landscape, many ideas come to mind and many need to be tried. The greater task is knowing what to eliminate in order to achieve a meaningful design with a minimum number of elements. Don't go overboard—too simplistic a plan can be boring. Variety in moderation is a sensible approach (*Figure 2.37*).

Figure 2.37—Know what to eliminate for an attractive design.

STEP 8. SELECTING PLANTS

In natural ecosystems, plants favor and thrive in one type of environment over another. Selecting plants for cultivation from environments similar to the landscape you are working with is a sound first step. The wider the gap there is between what the plants need and what the site or design allows, the greater the energy required to grow the plants. For example, if the landscape is in a semiarid climate, plants from semiarid regions are more likely to succeed than plants from humid environments. One then might conclude that the best plants to use are those that are indigenous to the area. In many cases, this is true. And, if this approach were taken

more often—and not the exception as it is in most cities—landscapes would probably consume fewer resources, maintain the integrity unique to the area, and foster a greater awareness of and appreciation for the natural world. However, most of us live in urban/suburban environments designed out of context with the natural region. From city to city throughout temperate North America, our urban and suburban environments are all too similar, using the same plant palette regardless of natural environmental conditions (*Figure 2.38*).

Knowing how climate strongly determines the natural potential of any land, and understanding where plants naturally grow and what they need can result in more compatible plant selection and placement and the efficient use of resources to maintain them (see Chapter I). Familiarity with soil and its characteristics (see Chapter III) and microclimates is necessary for putting this knowledge to use. Plant selection and placement are two of the most important aspects of finalizing your design. Plants that prefer moisture should be planted where the soil stays moist and cooler longer, where there is afternoon shade, and where there is available moisture from a high water table or water runoff from adjacent areas. Situate plants that prefer dry soil and sun away from structures of shade and where there is less water runoff from adjacent areas. Following the above recommendations does save water.

Although thousands of plant species have been identified, only a small percentage of them are actually in cultivation. Those that are, gen-erally are "mesic" (moist soil) plants native to humid environments. In fact, if you surveyed the temperate zones of North America, Europe, and Asia, regardless of the area's natural rainfall and amount of sunshine, you would find many of the same plants being used for landscapes in both humid and arid climates. These include ash, maple, forsythia, juniper, Kentucky bluegrass, and many more. On the other hand, it is difficult to find any "xeric" (dry soil) plants used across the country in a like manner. This is partly because mesic plants have been cultivated longer, people are more familiar with them, they are faster growing, and accessible irrigation is a given in many landscapes. However, mesic plants cannot withstand internal water deficits. Growing them in areas with low relative humidity and precipitation requires irrigation. Choices for landscapes of drier regions are to either use supplemental water and suffer higher

Figure 2.38—Most landscapes are designed out of context with the regional environment. Note red maple in Denver (left) as well as in Boston (right).

Figure 2.39—There are many xeric plants that are attractive, yet tolerate low relative humidity and low precipitation.

water bills, or select plants that are better adapted to the site and region. The latter is preferred if you want a landscape that uses less water. Many mesic plants (those that grow in moist soil) exhibit attractive form, flowers, fruits, and fall color and foliage. Equally, there are many xeric plants (those that grow in drier soil), especially shrubs and herbaceous perennials, with characteristics that are equally attractive (*Figure 2.39*). In addition, these plants are better equipped to tolerate low relative humidity, low natural rainfall, bright sunshine and drier soil.

Plants can be selected based on the natural precipitation of the area. For example, if you live in an area with 15 inches of precipitation per year, the plants you select should thrive in areas and sites with similar natural precipitation. These plants may need (a) little or no added water, (b) supplemental water only in a very dry year, or some may need (c) irrigation under av-

Figure 2.40—Look to dry-facing slopes for plants that tolerate dry soil.

erage precipitation to prevent them from going dormant under unusually dry conditions. If you do select plants that require supplemental irrigation to survive, there are many ways to conserve water (review Step 6 of this chapter).

For a landscape designed to reduce maintenance and the depletion of resources, group plants with similar cultural needs such as soil pH, light requirements, and water. The needs should be assessed for above and below ground parts. It is below the soil line where the competition for water and nutrients occur.

USING NATURE AS YOUR GUIDE

Knowing what conditions a plant prefers for optimum growth is difficult to ascertain unless the plant has a long history of cultivation under a variety of conditions. When you try to grow a plant without much information on its growing needs, use nature as your guide. Find out where the plant naturally grows and under what conditions. For example, if you want to plant Gambel oak (*Quercus Gambelii*), you can learn that it grows in the foothills and canyons in rocky soil, usually in full sun. In your landscape, you have a sunny, south-facing slope with good drainage. Gambel oak might be a suitable choice, providing it also satisfies the design function. For landscapes with low temperature hardiness, select plants native to northern areas that are adapted to colder temperatures. For plants tolerant of dry soil and cold temperature, look to the high deserts and west-facing slopes of mountainous areas (*Figure 2.40*).

In nature, plants take care of themselves, and in cultivation, we take care of them. The greater the discrepancy between the growing site and the plant's natural environment, the greater the maintenance and resources to grow them will likely be. Aspens are brilliant at high elevations where soil is moist, evenings are cool, and moisture is adequate. At lower elevations they are vulerable to leaf spot, galls, and other pests, exhibit disappointing fall color, and are short-lived (refer back to Figure 1.8).

At times, selecting plants can be frustrating, especially for those very difficult spots where choices are limited. For example, narrow spaces in full shade without irrigation that could use a tall screen. In this situation, you may need to find another use for the particular space or rethink the priorities and needs that you listed at the beginning of the design process.

NATIVE PLANTS

Interest in native plants is growing. The question is—what is native? Native plants in this handbook are defined as those species that over thousands of years have evolved and adapted to specific environments and geographic regions. Because of this, they are better equipped to tolerate the regional climate and local conditions.

In some instances, it is difficult to tell what is native to an area and what has been introduced either intentionally by humans or by default through transportation. (For example, seeds may hitch a ride on vehicles, the backs of animals, or plants may be transported from one area to another intentionally by humans.) The problem with using some nonnative species (exotics) is the associated risk of them escaping cultivation, invading natural ecosystems, and then outcompeting native plants. Russian olive and purple loosestrife are two nonnatives now considered to be noxious weeds in most temperate zone states. Native species and wildlife evolve together. When native plants cannot compete with the invasive nonnatives, many birds, small mammals, and insects lose their food source. Because of this, some wildlife may become threatened or at risk, and the altered plant community lacks diversity and, hence, becomes more susceptible to disease. Any time land is disturbed, the aggressive exotic species can proliferate without competition. Eliminating "weeds" in the landscape is very costly and time-consuming. However, of the many plants introduced into cultivation, few actually "escape" and become naturalized.

For regionally sensitive, more ecological landscapes, cultivating native species makes sense. They require less maintenance, have fewer insect and disease problems, are more adaptable to unpredictable weather patterns, natural precipitation, and relative humidity, and they help to maintain the integrity of the region.

Natives may not be for you. Using native plants solely and achieving true sustainability as we find in natural ecosystems is difficult, especially where there is so much human interference. For other landscape styles and approaches, there are many nonnative species that will suit the design and site. Landscaping for water conservation can be achieved regardless.

In the past, few native plants have been available at nurseries. However, over the last ten years, availability and variety have increased. This is an exciting time to investigate and experiment with new introductions suitable for your region.

PLANT SELECTION EXERCISE

The following exercise lists questions you might ask yourself when reviewing and checking your plant selections. Respond to the questions as you identify each plant choice.

1. What does the design call for? *Example: The design calls for privacy.*
2. What function does the plant have? *Example: The plant is to act as a screen.*
3. What plant did you select? *Example: New Mexican privet.*
4. Does the plant meet the design function? *Example: Yes.*
5. What kind of growing conditions does the plant need? *Example: It will tolerate moist, well-drained to dry soil in full sun.*
6. Does the site meet these conditions? *Example: Yes, the area is not irrigated but will receive irrigation runoff from adjacent areas.*
7. What is the plant's growth potential? *Example: The plant can grow up to 15 feet tall over time.*

TABLE 2.2 SAMPLE INVENTORY OF PLANTS

Plant type	Quantity	Location
Large trees	3 $1\frac{1}{2}$ " diameter	north side
Small trees	5 #5 containers	front yard
Large shrubs	5 #1 containers	backyard
Small shrubs	12 #3 containers	front yard
Vines	3 #1 containers	
Ground covers	300 bare root 500 $2\frac{1}{4}$" containers	front back
Herbaceous plants	to be decided later	

8. Does the site allow for its growth potential? *Example: Yes, it can grow to 10 feet and then it will need periodic pruning.*
9. What are the plant's aesthetic qualities? *Example: It has yellow flowers in spring and blue fruit in summer.*
10. Will you be able to enjoy these attributes? *Example: Yes, I can see the plant from my bedroom window.*
11. Is the plant available and in what form and size? *Example: Yes, both male and female plants are available in number one and number five containers.*
12. Is it affordable? *Example: Yes, as I plan to use small plants that I plant myself.*

TAKING INVENTORY OF THE PLANTS

In the final phase of plant selection, take an inventory of what you need. For example, your plan may have called for two large shade trees (50 feet tall by 30 feet wide), five medium-size–needle evergreens used as a screen, and one ground cover 2 feet high that will cover 30 square feet. Once the list is complete, review the designated planting areas for each by evaluating the growing conditions (e.g., 10 feet wide, dry, rocky soil, south exposure, full sun, pH 7.5). Make a list of plants that meet these requirements, along with several alternatives. Nursery catalogs, cooperative extension service recommended plant lists, and books and magazines focusing on your area are excellent sources of plant information.

TREES IN THE LANDSCAPE

In your design, the trees should be selected first. They constitute the biggest monetary commitment, will form the dominant structure, and will have the greatest impact upon the overall plan. They provide shade and physical comfort, enframement, screening, wildlife habitat, and various aesthetic amenities. They can also increase property values. Trees are dynamic, continually growing and changing as the seasons progress. And the environment changes with them. Consider your selections carefully and plant trees for posterity. Many generations will be affected by your decisions.

Deciduous trees naturally grow in forests in humid environments where water is available year-round, either from precipitation or underground sources. Unlike herbaceous plants whose aerial parts die to the ground, trees are continually exposed to sun, wind, rain, ice, and snow, and they constantly lose water through their leaves, buds, and stems. Many conifers store water in their trunk sapwood. If transpiration exceeds the water supply from the roots, trees tap their internal storage sites. Conifers as a rule tolerate dry soil better than deciduous trees.

To grow, trees need water. When cultivating them in semiarid and arid regions where natural precipitation is inadequate, we need to provide supplemental irrigation, especially during dry months (including winter). In your design, you can reduce their demands by reducing evaporation and transpiration. Grouping trees together will enable them to shade each other and thus increase the relative humidity. In addition, allowing leaf litter to remain as a mulch reduces soil evaporation (similar to a forest).

Figure 2.41—American holly, a broadleaf evergreen tree (left). Rocky Mountain juniper, a narrow-leaf evergreen tree (right).

Evergreen trees

Evergreen plants are those that lose only some of their leaves at a time (Figure 2.41). Their physical appearance generally remains consistent year-round. The leaves may be broad or very narrow like needles or scales. Most needle evergreens such as spruce, fir, arborvitae, and pine grow where temperatures are cool and winter moisture takes the form of snow. Most needle or scalelike plants are evergreens. Broadleaf evergreens such as citrus, fig, and mango grow where temperatures are warm and precipitation comes as rain. Few broadleaf evergreen trees are cold hardy in temperate zones, however, there are a number of broadleaf evergreen shrubs that are.

Needles and scaly leaves are very narrow and small. If the overall foliage is thick, as it is with junipers and spruce, the plants absorb light and assume a dark, dense appearance. This connotes a heaviness in the landscape, especially where they have been overplanted. Evergreens make strong textural statements especially in winter and are best planted in small groups. Spruce, Douglas fir and other fir, and some pine naturally grow where summers are short and winters are long and cold with persistent snow cover. They grow well in microclimates where the soil is cool and moist, such as northern exposure, but still need sun. Junipers, Arizona cypress, and piñon pine are usually found in drier areas on hilltops or on south-facing slopes with less accumulated soil moisture. In the landscape, they prefer full sun with warm, well-drained soil. They thrive in microclimates where soils are drier, such as southern or western exposures or in coarse, rocky soil. Evergreens are often used as windbreaks, screens, and background plantings.

Deciduous trees

Deciduous plants lose all their leaves at one time. Their winter and summer appearances are starkly contrasted. Deciduous broadleaf trees grow in temperate zones where precipitation comes in the form of rain or snow, and they make

Figure 2.42—Forest of deciduous trees: oak, maple, ash, and elm.

Figure 2.43—Xeric tall shrub (New Mexican privet) can be used as a small tree.

up the bulk of our urban shade trees, such as maple, oak, ash, and elm (Figure 2.42).

Leaves come in various sizes and shapes and display a fine, moderate, or coarse texture. Trees with fine to moderate textures provide filtered or dappled shade. Large or denser foliage creates heavy shade and makes it difficult for plants to survive underneath it. Deciduous trees indicate seasonal changes with flowers, fruits, and fall color—all important considerations for a landscape with year-round interest. Large broadleaf trees are recommended for providing shade in summer and sun in winter.

SHRUBS IN THE LANDSCAPE

In natural ecosystems, shrub vegetation is usually an accurate gauge of distinct wet and dry seasons. Shrubs grow sparsely in some places or can be impenetrable in others (depending on the amount of moisture). Thicket-forming deciduous shrubs prosper in areas with cold winters and hot summers. Broadleaf evergreen shrubs (chaparral) dominate where summers are hot and dry and winters are cool and moist. Many xeric shrubs from arid regions develop long roots, enabling them to survive on less moisture than trees because they have less bulk to support. Shrub lands (natural areas dominated by shrubs) may coexist with woodlands or replace them on dry, rocky slopes. In the natural world, xeric shrubs will flourish on sites too dry for woodlands and too rocky for grasses.

Shrubs exhibit characteristics similar to trees. In some cases, the difference between a shrub and tree can be very vague. Generally, shrubs range in height from less than 1 foot to more than 15 feet, and with multiple stems from their base. The advantage shrubs have over trees in a landscape design is that they come from a wider variety of environments—from very dry to very moist, very warm to very cold. This versatility translates to more plant choices for arid and semiarid landscapes. Some shrubs can be grown as ornamental trees on small properties, others make great accents. Many can be used as screens, borders, ground covers, and shelter or habitats for wildlife. It is easier to design a low-water-use landscape using shrubs in place of trees—it boils down to plant choice (Figure 2.43).

Xeric shrubs are common in deserts. Deserts are difficult to classify because they vary from region to region. However, they do have several things in common. They are areas with limited rainfall and where evaporation is excessive. Precipitation is low, irregular, and unreliable, relative humidity is low, and temperatures are high during the day and cool down at night. Deserts boast few cloudy days with intense sunlight. When moisture does arrive, it often falls during one season, most often winter. Sometimes (as in the Sonoran Desert) it may fall in the summer as well. The amount of potential transpiration from plants increases with the temperature, but desert shrubs have evolved some interesting adaptations and intriguing forms that withstand water deficits. Some may have small or no leaves; others may have succulent stems or leaves or roots that penetrate 15 feet plus. Others adapt by dropping their leaves during the dry spells and leafing out when it rains. Desert plants are generally low in stature and, because of competition for water, are widely spaced. Many lie dormant throughout most of the year. The desert landscape is unique to the desert. If this is where you live, take advantage of its beauty *(Figure 2.44)*.

VINES IN THE LANDSCAPE

Vines offer an excellent means of creating vertical emphasis in the landscape. Before making a selection, know their growing patterns, cultural needs, and what they can provide. Vines grow one of three ways. Some climb and support themselves by attaching small, holdfast appendages or rootlets to walls such as Virginia creeper and English ivy *(Figure 2.45)*. Others have modified leaves called tendrils that they use to cling to other supports. Peas and clematis are two examples. The third type, such as bittersweet, grows by twining and twisting its woody stem. Many vines will also sprawl along the ground, mounding on themselves. Some (such as Japanese honeysuckle) can be useful for preventing steep banks from eroding.

HERBACEOUS PLANTS IN THE LANDSCAPE

Herbaceous plants are not woody. They die down to the ground in winter, and some go dormant in summer. Many can withstand the heat and dry soil of arid regions. Herbaceous plants may be perennial; their tops die back each season but growth is renewed the following spring. Biennials sprout leafy growth the first year, flower and fruit the second year, and then they die. Annual herbaceous plants complete their entire life cycle in one growing season and then they die as well.

Herbaceous perennials are from a wide variety of environments (from wet to dry) and habitats, including forests, woodlands, shrub

Figure 2.44—*The unique beauty of a desert.*

Figure 2.45—*Virginia creeper vine attaches and climbs by small holdfasts.*

lands, prairies, tundra, and wetlands. Ranging in size from a few inches high to over 15 feet, herbaceous plants provide a variety of colors and textures for the garden. Many are also useful as ground covers where they can be positioned to unify the landscape design, shade the soil, reduce water use, yet still require little maintenance *(Figure 2.46)*. Some herbaceous plants

Figure 2.46—Herbaceous plants provide a variety of colors and textures (cowboy's delight and aster).

Figure 2.47—Many plants, such as groundsel, needle, and thread grass, are more attractive together than apart.

that are perennial in mild climates can be grown as annuals in colder areas.

Some perennials are best used alone (crambe and ravenna grass) where their coarse, commanding presence makes a statement. Some have delicate foliage (astilbe and threadleaf coreopsis) and are best used en masse. Many herbaceous plants interact well with other plants. Indian paintbrush paired with sagebrush, groundsel, or needle and thread grass is an attractive as well as symbiotic combination (*Figure 2.47*).

Many herbaceous perennials are native to semiarid and arid environments or adapt well to dry conditions. Their versatility and variation equal the beauty of better known flowering plants from humid climates. As with shrubs, using less water in a perennial garden depends on your choice of plants. A landscape design incorporating perennials suited to the regional climate creates a landscape that portrays a rich, natural character. Penstemon with piñon pine and junipers clearly define a western landscape, just as maple and beech identify an eastern one. Using plants suited to the region is an affirmation of the region's inherent beauty (*Figure 2.48*).

Herbaceous plants are also prevalent in the tundra of polar and subarctic climates. Tundra is devoid of trees, but consists of lichens, grasses, sedges, flowering plants, shrubby willows, and birch. It is characterized by long, cold winters and short summers. The same vegetation that inhabits the far north is also found on the

Figure 2.48—Landscapes for arid regions.

tops of mountains. Although gardening is not a common pastime in the tundra, the natural landscape inspires endless ideas for rock/alpine gardens. The tasteful use of rocks in a landscape interjects cool, moist, shady, and sunny microclimates suitable for a variety of cushionlike plants from these areas.

GRASSES

Grasses are also herbaceous. They are found in every ecosystem at all latitudes, but are the dominant plant types in prairies and meadows. For grasslands to develop instead of forests, natural precipitation is limited to part of the year, resulting in both a moist and a dry season. Unlike trees, grasses are not woody and die back to the ground every year. During winter, more than half of the plant is hidden under the soil. Winter buds lie dormant near or below the soil surface, protected against water loss by dead plant material from the previous season. Water needs are minimal during the dormant season (usually late fall and winter), but throughout the growing season, grasses require moisture. (Many can tolerate summer drought from one to eight weeks.) Although boundaries are arbitrary, grasslands of semiarid climates are generally considered to collect half the amount of precipitation of humid climates (20 to 40 inches or more) with precipitation ranging between 8 to 15 inches per year, positioning grasslands between deserts and temperate deciduous forests. Using grasses in combination with wildflowers is an attractive and practical move away from traditional lawns to prairie or meadow landscapes that consume half the moisture.

Primarily sun loving, grasses comprise one of the most widespread and most adaptable groups of plants. They have long supplied much of our food (wheat, rice, corn) and lawns. Now, they are being used as ornamentals as well. The attraction of ornamental grasses for gardeners is in part due to their interesting foliage, unique flowers, winter form, and tolerance to various growing environments.

Figure 2.49—Ornamental grasses can jazz up any garden.

Not only are they able to withstand summer heat and dry soil, but they also attract few pests and require little maintenance most of the year. Ornamental grasses range in size from a few inches to 20 feet tall. Serviceable in narrow spaces, they can jazz up perennial flower gardens, and lend interest near ponds and in containers (*Figure 2.49*).

LAWNS

What is a lawn? A lawn is uniformly maintained turf grass consisting of thousands of grass plants tightly meshed together, appearing and acting as one. As a unit, it figures prominently in our human habitats. It moderates temperature, controls soil erosion, traps dust, reduces glare, and offers human comfort and pleasure. A lawn in a sunny area is 10°F cooler than bare soil and up to 30° cooler than concrete or asphalt. It is hard to fault lawns when they provide so much. Yet, maintaining them as we have in the past is contrary to water conservation. When it is actively growing, Kentucky bluegrass (or other cool-season turf grasses) needs between 1–1$\frac{1}{2}$ inches of water per week. In a cool, humid climate that receives 20 to 40 inches of precipitation per year, rainfall may provide most of these water needs. In semiarid or arid environments with less than 15 inches of precipitation per year, the difference has to be made up by other means. Because of this, Kentucky bluegrass and other cool-season

Figure 2.50—A warm-season buffalo grass lawn requires less water in summer than Kentucky bluegrass.

lawns are major water consumers in semiarid to arid landscapes. While it is true that with irrigation coupled with other cultural practices such as fertilization we can grow a near-perfect lawn in most environments, it is impractical, expensive, and wasteful to do so when our natural resources are shrinking because of greater demands from growing populations and development. We can help by reducing the size of lawns, selecting turf grasses better suited to the environment, and by becoming more efficient with our irrigation systems and general water use.

Cool- and warm-season grasses

In the landscape, we recognize two types of turf grasses: cool- and warm-season. Kentucky bluegrass, fescue, and perennial rye are examples of cool-season grasses. Buffalo and blue grama grass are examples of warm-season grasses.

Plants experience two types of dormancy: one in response to cold temperatures and the other in response to a lack of moisture. Dormancy does not mean "dead," it means "resting stage" in which there is little biological activity. Outwardly it appears as if the plant has stopped growing. In summer without moisture, cool-season grasses will go dormant and become brown. We rarely see this because our lawns are usually irrigated. In winter, cool-season grasses generally become semidormant and turn a dull green, rarely brown. This is in part because they are not usually fully dormant. Warm-season grasses undergo full dormancy in winter, turning an attractive golden to tannish brown. We can also see dormancy occur in summer if they become water stressed. In most semiarid and arid regions, we are growing cool-season grasses that require $1–1^1/_2$ inches of water per week to keep them green. Warm-season grasses require only about one-third as much. We are not used to nor are we comfortable with seeing our lawns brown in winter or summer, so we irrigate. The problem with lawns today is not necessarily the grass itself, but the type of grass used. To conserve water, you may want to change the plant type, not necessarily eliminate the lawn. Check with your cooperative extension service for recommendations for your area (*Figure 2.50*).

Cool-season grasses

Most cool-season grasses that comprise lawns originally came from the forest margins of Europe and Asia, where precipitation is well distributed throughout the year. Their seeds germinate between 60 to 85°F and their optimum growth temperature is between 60 to 75°F. Cool-season grasses grow best in spring and fall and go dormant in summer when soil water content is deficient. In winter, they do not generally go fully dormant because their root systems continue to grow as long as soil temperatures remain above freezing. Because of this, they often maintain a dull green color. In summer, under heat stress and without irrigation, their root growth slows down and, in some cases, may disintegrate as the plants go dormant. However, full dormancy is rarely seen if these grasses are irrigated. Although cool-season grasses tolerate drought by going dormant, they cannot tolerate dry periods as long as warm-season grasses can. If water is not available, they eventually die.

Types of cool-season grasses

Kentucky bluegrass, the most commonly used cool-season turf grass in North America, emigrated from Europe and North Africa. It first made its way to this country as a passenger in hay on ships that were bringing supplies to America. Grass seeds began to germinate and establish themselves in fields. Virginians began to sow it in the grainfields among the other crops. The seeds began to disperse and when forests were cleared, the grass moved in. Later, missionaries helped to spread it throughout the Ohio River Valley. In the mid-1800s, Kentucky bluegrass became the "the front lawn" and a symbol of the American suburban landscape.

Kentucky bluegrass is a medium-textured cool-season rhizomatous grass valued for its rich green foliage, soft, cool feel, and recuperative powers if injured. Functionally it is suited to high foot traffic and recreation. However, growing it in sandy or compacted soil, fast-draining sites such as slopes, berms or mounds, hot areas such as west- or south-facing slopes, or areas with reflected heat from asphalt, concrete, and buildings will require more water use than necessary.

It is difficult to find a lawn grass as versatile and as functional as Kentucky bluegrass. Most recently, tall fescue was thought to be a good substitute. Tall fescue is a coarse-textured cool-season bunchgrass (although there are varieties with finer texture). It provides a more vigorous, heat-and-cold–tolerant lawn with lower fertilizer requirements than Kentucky bluegrass. It grows in sun and some shade and can develop very deep roots in loam or amended clay. Most research shows that although tall fescue can withstand longer periods of time without water than Kentucky bluegrass (because of its more aggressive root system), overall it uses nearly the same amount.

Cool-season grasses should be grown on fairly level ground or gentle, north-facing slopes with good drainage and preferably in loamy soil, 8 to 12 inches deep.

Warm-season grasses

Warm-season grasses used as lawn boast a more diverse origin than cool-season grasses. Many originated in warmer climates such as Africa, South America, and Asia, and eventually migrated northward. Generally, warm-season grasses have deeper root systems than the cool-season varieties (in cultivation, this may depend on the soil), and are more tolerant of dry soil, warm temperatures, and low relative humidity.

Figure 2.51—Comparison between warm-season grasses (front) and cool-season grasses (back) in early spring.

Seeds germinate between 70 to 95°F, with their optimum growth occurring between 80 to 95°F. Warm-season grasses go dormant more readily in cold temperatures than cool-season species and begin to discolor as cold temperatures set in. Once a hard frost occurs, a clear distinction between cool-season and warm-season grasses can be made, because warm-season grasses are fully dormant and turn a golden brown while the cool-season varieties remain green. Warm-season grass roots also go dormant, even if soil temperatures are near 32°F. And in the summer, under very dry conditions, they can go dormant, despite the fact they require less water for active growth than cool-season grasses. However, warm-season grasses are better able to withstand dryness for longer periods of time (about three times longer) than cool-season grasses. Once moistened, they resume growth (Figure 2.51).

Types of warm-season grasses

Blue grama is a warm-season bunchgrass that grows 10 to 16 inches tall. It may become clumpy if severely heat or drought stressed. In nature, it is found in association with buffalo grass in short- and mid-grass prairies. The two are often grown together in cultivation.

Buffalo grass is a sod-forming grass that is becoming more popular. Several varieties are currently available. It makes an attractive turf, grows 6 inches tall, can be left unmowed, and may only need 1 to 2 inches of water every three to four weeks during the growing season.

Bermuda grass is quite aggressive and can invade other areas, but it is also tolerant of heat, drought, and salt. Cold, dry winters limit its use, although some varieties adapted for cold temperatures are available. Warm-season grasses may not be cold hardy for your region. Bermuda and Zoysia are less hardy than blue grama and buffalo. Check with your cooperative extension service for recommendations for your area.

PLANT SIZE AND PURCHASE

Because there are so many plants to choose from, it is usually not difficult to find a plant that meets your height, size, spread, aesthetic, and cultural specifications. As you make your final selections, choose the most dominant plants first. The order usually starts with trees (sometimes lawns), followed by shrubs, ground covers, and then flowering and other herbaceous plants. All plants other than shade trees should be considered at their mature size. With larger trees, it is useful to view them in ten-year growth increments, ultimately planning for two-thirds their mature size. This will help you plan for changes that occur when sunny areas become shady and other plants alter their performance as the trees grow.

What size should you buy? Size depends on price, growth rate, what you can physically handle, how it is grown (bareroot, balled and burlapped, or container), and availability. Smaller trees generally transplant better and are quicker to establish. Trees with greater than a $2^1/_2$-inch trunk diameter are more difficult to handle and take longer to establish. Faster growing plants can be purchased in smaller sizes, whereas, you may want to buy slower growing ones such as conifers in larger sizes. Plants that are more sensitive to dry air and winds should have a substantial root system. In this case, a larger size may be safer. (Plants that are more vulnerable to winds are often from humid environments; their foliage may be thin without a hairy or waxy covering.) Money is usually a primary concern. Balance your plant budget and buy slower growing plants in large sizes and faster growing ones in small sizes (see Table 2.2).

Phase V: Drawing the Final Plan

This is it—you have spent many hours getting to this stage. Congratulations. You are ready to finish your composition. Before you draw any final plans, you may find it helpful to fashion mock-ups of your design. You can use cardboard, newspaper, boxes, chairs, tables, strings, hoses, even balloons to represent the various elements in your design. Strings or watering hoses are good for marking bed lines and paths on the ground. Walk around the various elements and proposed paths to see if they will work and feel right. Always keep safety in mind.

When you are satisfied with your decisions and comfortable with the plan, draw it to scale in its final form on durable, reproducible paper such as vellum. This final drawing should show details of the elements and how they relate to each other. You should specify plants, their location, spacing, and quantity. Identify structural materials as well, including paths, fences, patios, and benches.

If the drawing has the potential for getting too cluttered and difficult to read, some details such as plant selection and placement can be drawn on another piece of paper. All these final drawings will be valuable for your records, whether you implement your design yourself or if you contract the work out to others (*Figure 2.52a & Figure 2.52b*).

Phase VI: Estimating Costs

For an estimate as to what your landscape design will cost, use your plan to list expenses. Costs include materials such as plants, walls, paths, irrigation, and lighting as well as labor, removal, and dump fees. The size of the plants and how they are packaged affect the price.

Bareroot plants and containers are usually less expensive than balled and burlapped ones, but so much of this depends on the type and size of plant. Other costs include demolition, removal, dumping, and storage. You can list the items by quantity, square footage and/or linear feet. Call nurseries, hardware stores, and contractors to get an idea of the dollar amount involved (*Table 2.3*).

Phase VII: Implementing the Plan

Implementing the design is an orderly process. The first activities undertaken should be those that cause the most disruption or damage. These include using heavy equipment, traffic and soil compaction, constructing rock walls and paths, installing main irrigation lines, and any electrical

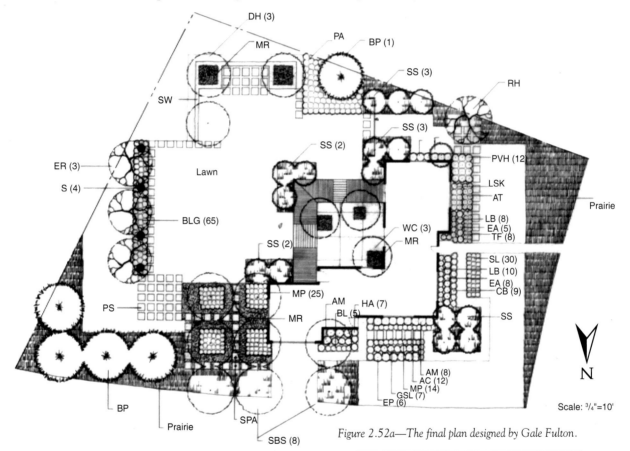

Figure 2.52a—The final plan designed by Gale Fulton.

Code	Qty.	Latin Name	Common Name				
AC	12	Aquilegia caerulea	Rocky Mountain Columbine	LB	18	Schizachyrium scoparium	Little Bluestem
AM	12	Acanthus spinosus	Spiny Bear's breeches	LSK	10	Liatris spicata 'Kobold'	Gayfeather
AT	10	Asclepias tuberosa	Butterfly Milkweed	MP	14	Oenothera missouriensis	Missouri Primrose
BC	5	Bergenia cordifolia	Pigsqueak Plant	Mps	100	Matteucia pensylvanica	Ostrich Fern
BLG	65	Elymus arenarius	Blue Lyme Grass	PA	60	Pennisetum alopecuroides	Fountain Grass
BP	5	Pinus aristata	Bristlecone Pine	PS			Paving Stone (Blue Stone)
CB	9	Heuchera sanguinea	Coral Bells	PVH	18	Panicum virgatum 'Heavy Metal'	'Heavy Metal' Switch Grass
DH	3	Crataegus mollis	Downy Hawthorn	RH	1	Crataegus ambiguus	Russian Hawthorn
EA	13	Epilobium angustifolium	Fireweed	SL	30	Sencio longilobus	Longleaf Goundsel
EP	6	Echinacea purpurea	Purple Cone Flower	SS	16	Rhus glabra	Smooth Sumac
ER	3	Cercis canadensis	Eastern Redbud	TE	8	Thelesperma filifolia	Threadleaf Thelesperma
HA	7	Heuchera americana	Purple Coral Bells	WC	1	Malus 'Echtemeyer'	Weeping Crab

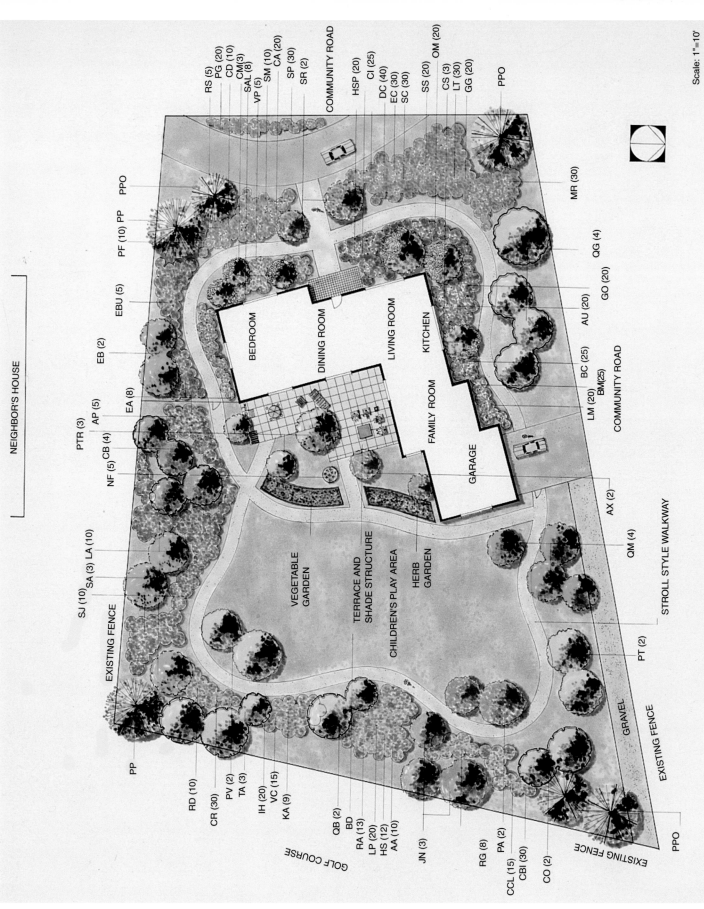

Figure 2.52b. The final plan—a different style designed by Nobuo Iwata.

PLANT LIST

	Latin Name	Common Name	Code	Size	Quantity
DECIDUOUS TREES	Amelanchier xgrandiflora	Apple Shadbush	AX	12'	2
	Carpinus betulus	European Hornbeam	CB	12'	4
	Catalpa speciosa	Northern Catalpa	CS	12'	3
	Celtis occidentalis	Common Hackberry	CO	10'	2
	Crataegus mollis	Downy Hawthorn	CM	10'	3
	Euonymus bungeanus	Winterberry Euonymus	EB	10'	2
	Juglans nigra	Black Walnut	JN	12'	3
	Populus tremuloides	Quaking Aspen	PTR	15'	3
	Prunus armeniaca	Apricot	PA	12'	2
	Prunus virginiana	Chokecherry	PV	12'	2
	Ptelea trifoliata	Hop Tree	PT	12'	2
	Quercus bicolor	Swamp White Oak	QB	15'	2
	Quercus gambelii	Gambel's Oak	QG	15'	4
	Quarcus macrocarpa	Bur Oak	QM	12'	4
	Sorbus alnifolia	Korean MountainAsh	SA	12'	3
	Syringa reticulata	Japanese Tree Lilac	SR	10'	2
	Tilia americana	Americana Linden	TA	12'	3
EVERGREEN TREES	Picea pungens	Colorado Spruce	PP	12'	2
	Pinus ponderosa	Ponderosa Pine	PPO	12'	4
SHRUBS	Aesculus pavia	Red Buckeye	AP	5-Gal	5
	Amelanchier alnifolia	Native Serviceberry	AA	5-Gal	10
	Caryopteris xclandonensis	Blue Mist Spirea	CCL	5-Gal	15
	Cotoneaster divaricatus	Spreading Cotoneaster	CD	5-Gal	10
	Euonymus alatus	Winged Euonymus	EA	5-Gal	8
	Euonymus bungeanus	Winterberry Euonymus	EBU	5-Gal	5
	Hibiscus syriacus	Rose of Sharon	HS	5-Gal	12
	Kolkwitzia amabilis	Beautybush	KA	5-Gal	9
	Lonicera alpigena	Alps Honeysuckle	LA	5-Gal	10
	Potentilla fruticosa	Bush Cinquefoil	PF	5-Gal	10
	Rhamnus smithii	Smith Buckthorn	RS	5-Gal	5
	Ribes aureum	Golden Current	RA	5-Gal	13
	Rubus deliciosus	Boulder Raspberry	RD	5-Gal	10
	Spiraea japonica	Japanese Spirea	SJ	5-Gal	10
	Symphoricarpos albus	White Snowberry	SAL	5-Gal	8
	Syringa meyeri	Meyer Lilac	SM	5-Gal	10
	Viburnum carlesii	Korean Spice Viburnum	VC	5-Gal	15
	Viburnum plicatum tomentosum	Double File Viburnum	VP	5-Gal	5
PERENNIALS	Callirhoe involucrata	Wine Cup	CI	Flats	25
	Campanula rotundifolia	Bluebell	CR	Flats	30
	Hemerocallis species	Daylily	HSP	Flats	20
	Iris hybrids	Bearded Iris	IH	Flats	20
	Linum perenne var. Lewisii	Blue Flax	LP	Flats	20
	Oenothera missouriensis	Ozark Sundrop	OM	Flats	20
GROUND COVER	Delosperma cooperi	Pink Hardy Ice Plant	DC	1-Gal	40
	Delosperma nubigenum	Hardy Yellow Ice Plant	DN	1-Gal	40
	Galium odoratum	Sweet Woodruff	GO	1-Gal	20
	Lamium maculatum	SpottedDead Nettle	LM	1-Gal	20
	Mahonia repens	Creeping Grape Holly	MR	Flats	30
	Santolina chamaecyparissus	Lavender Cotton	SC	1-Gal	30
	Sedum spurium	Two-row Stonecrop	SS	1-Gal	20
ORNAMENTAL	Calamagrostis acutiflora	Karl Foerster Feather Reed Grass	CA	Flats	20
	Nymphaeà Firecrest	Firecrest	NF		5
LAWNS	Buchloe dactyloides	Buffalo Grass	BD		
ANNUALS	Cosmos bipinnatus	Cosmos	CBI	Flats	30
	Eschscholzia californica	California Poppy	EC	Flats	30
	Gomphrena globosa	Globe Amaranth	GG	Flats	20
	Portulaca grandiflora	Moss Rose	PG	Flats	20
	Lavatera trimestris	Annual Mallow	LT	Flats	30
	Sanvitalia procumbens	Creeping Zinnia	SP	Flats	30
SHADE PLANTS	Arctostaphylos uva-ursi	Kinnikinnick	AU	1-Gal	20
	Bergenia cordifolia	Heartleaf Bergenia	BC	1-Gal	25
	Brunnera macrophylla	Perennial Forget-me-not	BM	1-Gal	25

Notes:
1. Strolling walkway will be constructed using crushed gray gravel contained by a 4-inch concrete edger.
2. Irrigation for the site shall consist of an automatic irrigation system. The types shall vary using drip irrigation, pop-up spray and rotors, depending on the size of the site to be watered.
3. Planting beds along building shall be drip irrigated and plants installed 2 feet from the building.

TABLE 2.3 SAMPLE CHART FOR ESTIMATING COSTS				
Checklist of Expenses				
Item	Quantity	Unit Cost	Labor Cost	Total
demolition (e.g., removal of material)				
soil preparation amendments mulch fertilizer compost				
utilities (e.g., electrical service)				
structures (e.g., paths, fences, walkways, walls)				
trees shrubs ground covers perennials vines lawn seeds				
irrigation design materials installation construction planting				

work. Once earthmoving has been completed and all the hard surfaces and utilities are in place, soil preparation (see Chapter III on soil amendments), planting, final placement of irrigation heads, and mulching can follow.

When and how your design plan translates into reality depends on your time, energy, and money. What part of your landscape should be tackled first depends on what is most important to you. Decide what work you are willing to do and what you want done by others. Focus the various activities on the time of year when help is available and when it is best to do certain tasks (see Chapter V on planting). Adopt the attitude that the design can be done in stages. It doesn't have to happen all at one time. Up to now, you have put a lot of energy into the design process and there is a danger of becoming shortsighted. Continue to be flexible with your plan and willing to make changes when something doesn't work out exactly as planned.

CHAPTER III

Soil

Introduction

Soil is a facial cover—the earth's crust—that acts as a highway between life and death, land and atmosphere, and plants and animals. It also stores water, air, and nutrients and provides a medium for the exchange of elements and chemical reactions. Not all soils are the same nor do they have the same kind or numbers of microorganisms. Most are mineral soils with varying amounts of organic material derived from living organisms. Those with very high amounts of organic material (usually in association with water) are organic soils.

How do soils develop? Mineral soils start with rock that becomes subjected to the various influences of climate and other things such as chemical weathering and leaching, physical movement, vegetation, living organisms, and topography. Eventually rock breaks into smaller

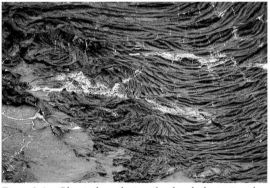

Figure 3.1—Chemical weathering of rock—the beginning of soil formation.

and smaller fragments, mixing with other materials such as remnants of living organisms. These tiny fragments and organic remains settle, organize, and become arranged into a soil profile *(Figure 3.1)*.

What is Soil? Is it

___ a. Animal

___ b. Vegetable

___ c. Mineral

✓ d. All of the above

Soil is an elaborate mixture of many things:

- A place where mineral particles from rocks and gravel, water, air, and dead and living organisms interact, break down and recombine;
- A graveyard where minerals are recycled for the renewal of others;
- A world where thousands of microorganisms live and most insects undergo a portion of their life cycle.

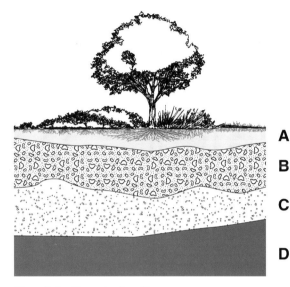

Figure 3.2—*General soil profile.*

A
B
C
D

The soil profile consists of a sequence of layers from the surface on down to bedrock. The model profile has four of these layers, each varying in thickness, color, texture, and composition. Realistically, some soils have all layers, while others may be lacking one or two. What layers are found and to what depth depends on the topography, region, and climate under which the soil develops. A diagram of the profile is illustrated in Figure 3.2. For convenience, each layer is labeled A, B, C, or D. This is not a taxonomic classification. The top layer (A) has the highest proportion of organic matter, microorganisms, insects, and earthworms. This is often referred to as "topsoil." The second layer (B) is mostly mineral matter derived from weathered rock and some materials of layer A. It is usually firmer than layer A and is often referred to as "subsoil." Both layers A and B are vital to root growth. The third layer (C) is parent or weathered material from which particles in A and B may or may not have come. Layer D is bedrock.

In Chapter I we learned that in nature, vegetation types (e.g., forests and grasslands) are expressions of climate. They are also expressions of the soil as shown in Figure 3.3. Soil and vegetation types correspond. For example, more mature, developed soil profiles are found in humid areas of deciduous forests and tall-grass prairies. Areas with large amounts of expansive clay are characteristic of short-grass prairies and semiarid shrub lands. Desert soil profiles reveal little of layer A because the breakdown of organic matter is so slow. Evergreen forests have more organic matter extending into layer B. Young soils and areas with unfriendly environments have poorly developed soil profiles, such as on high mountains, steep hillsides, and sand dunes. Areas with a deep organic layer (at least 12 inches) that develops when soil is saturated for at least one month out of the year are considered to be organic.

Different soils indicate which plants will grow best. For example, deciduous trees grow in moist, well-drained mineral soil with sufficient organic matter. To grow these trees in cultivation, it is best to try to provide similar conditions. This may not be easy because in cities and suburbia soil profiles are drastically different. Instead of taking thousands of years to develop, they can be totally transformed in a matter of days. The change is usually initiated when a backhoe removes the topsoil and stockpiles it for later use (*Figure 3.4*). Once the organic layer is removed, natural nutrient cycles are disrupted and soil organisms including earthworms are damaged or displaced. In addition, the heavy equipment and foot traffic compact the soil that remains, thus eliminating air spaces between soil particles and reducing oxygen levels necessary for healthy root growth. Ultimately, the soil left for landscaping is a haphazard recombination of ingredients, some of which are natural, and others that are foreign such as brick, asphalt, or other debris that occupies space where plant roots might grow (*Figure 3.5*). Instead of a continuum between layers as in a naturally developed soil, there are various vertical and horizontal obstructions consisting of sidewalks, streets, parking strips, driveways, and utility lines. Under these conditions, any benefit from weathering of the parent rock

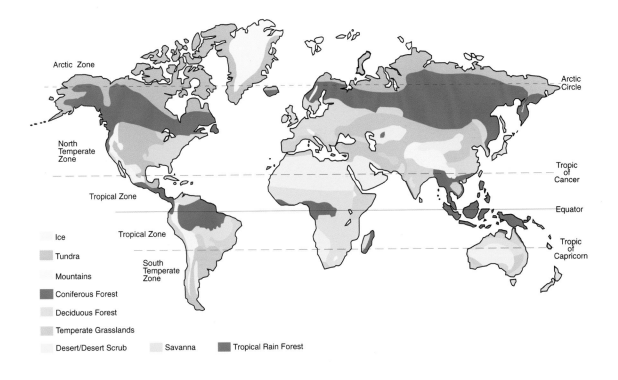

Arctic Zone

North
Temperate
Zone

Tropical Zone

Tropical Zone

South
Temperate
Zone

Arctic
Circle

Tropic
of
Cancer

Equator

Tropic
of
Capricorn

Ice

Tundra

Mountains

Coniferous Forest

Deciduous Forest

Temperate Grasslands

Desert/Desert Scrub   Savanna   Tropical Rain Forest

Rain forests
weathered soil,
high in clay,
low in organic matter and fertility due to rapid
  decomposition,
leaching and recyling of materials

Savannas and tropical grasslands
highly weathered,
low fertility,
easily worked

Mountainous soil
various,
immature,
poorly developed profile,
gravelly or stony

Tundra
high in organic matter,
subject to frost action,
underlain with permanent frost,
poorly developed profile

Coniferous forests
cool, temperate climates,
acidic with accumulated organic matter in subsoil,
low in fertility due to leaching,
glaciated areas

Deciduous broadleaf forests
cool, temperate, moist climate, mineral, moist soil,
little leaching,
moderately high fertility,
well-developed horizons,
only part of the organic matter is recycled annually

Grasslands
Tall- to mixed-grass prairie:
temperate, moist climate,
dark brown becoming lighter with depth,
high in organic matter, fertile

Mid- to tall-grass prairie:
temperate and tropical climates, moderate rainfall,
rich in organic matter,
most vegetable matter returned back to soil as organic
  residue,
relatively lower level of leaching, easily worked,
productive

Semiarid grassland:
sparse vegetation,
limited rainfall,
little organic matter and nitrogen,
horizons usually thin,
light rain results in high plant nutrients,
some areas with excessive amounts of soluble salts

Deserts
dry climate,
low precipitation, little leaching,
sparse vegetation,
low in organic matter,
poorly developed layers,
underlain with layer of cemented calcium carbonate

Figure 3.3—Vegetation is an expression of soil characteristics.

and the free flow of water and air in both directions is negligible. Roots grow unpredictably as they try, sometimes unsuccessfully, to find the paths of least resistance (*Figure 3.6*).

The success of your landscape is heavily dependent upon your soil. How plants perform and the many things you can do to encourage their growth (e.g., amendments, fertilizer, irrigation) depend on soil characteristics. The more you

Figure 3.4—Soil profile (A) and its destruction (B).

know about how your soil behaves, the easier the landscape will be to manage and the more successful your xeriscape will be.

Getting to Know Your Soil

All the components that comprise soil—organic and mineral materials, macro- and micro-organisms, plants, and chemicals—determine its ability to store water, nutrients, and air. Water, nutrients, and air are essential for plant growth whether in cultivation or in a naturalized setting. The degree to which the soil provides these ingredients will determine the plant's health and its efficient use of resources.

The following exercises are designed to help you become more knowledgeable about the soil on your site and what it is capable of. For exercises 1 through 6, you will need a shovel, a quart jar, two cups of dry soil dug 2 to 6 inches deep from the areas you want to test, a glass of water, dishwashing detergent, paper towels, and an optional PH soil kit. The exercises should be repeated at different locations throughout the landscape where the soil appears to differ.

Figure 3.5—Brick, asphalt, and other debris in the soil occupy valuable space for root growth.

Figure 3.6—Root growth is unpredictable.

EXERCISES ON SOIL TEXTURE

Figure 3.7—Feel the texture of your soil.

EXERCISE 1

This exercise enables you to feel and identify your soil's texture. From your sample, take a pinch of soil and work it between your fingers. Try to describe how it feels. Small particles have a finer, smoother feel than coarser ones. Larger, coarser particles feel abrasive and gritty. Sand has larger particles and feels harsher than silt or clay. Clay feels more powdery when dry *(Figure 3.7)*.

EXERCISE 2

Fill the jar with equal amounts of water and soil. Add one teaspoon of dishwashing detergent.

Figure 3.8—Sand particles will settle to the bottom, clay particles will rest on top.

Remove twigs, leaves, or other debris. With a tight lid on the jar, shake it vigorously. Place the jar where it will be undisturbed for thirty-six hours until the particles settle. Larger pieces of sand will settle to the bottom within minutes. Silt will settle within the hour. Clay particles will settle in the next one to two days, though some clay may remain in suspension indefinitely. While the particles are settling, proceed to the next experiment *(Figure 3.8)*.

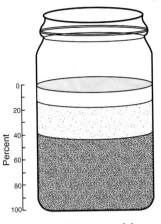

Figure 3.9—Measure each layer of all the solid materials.

Thirty-six hours later

Note the layers in the jar. Measure the total height of all the solid materials and then measure each distinct layer. Divide each layer by the total and multiply by 100 to obtain the percentage *(Figure 3.9)*. Plot the percentages of each layer on the triangle and connect them with a dotted line. Note where they intersect for soil texture *(Figure 3.10)*.

The basic building blocks of most soils are mineral particles. This exercise will help you identify the different mineral particles in your soil sample. Mineral particles (those that can pass through a 2 mm sieve) include sand, silt, and clay. Gravel is more than 2 mm in diameter; sand particles are between 2 to .05 mm and can be seen with the naked eye. Silt particles are very small—.05 to .002 mm—and can be seen only under a microscope. Clay particles are even smaller, less than .002 mm *(Figure 3.11)*. A millimeter equals .0394 of an inch. The size of these particles and their proportions determine the

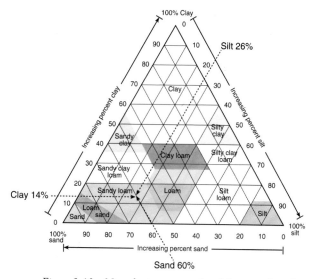

Figure 3.10—Note the percentage of each layer on the soil texture triangle.

soil's ability to retain moisture, air, and nutrients for plant use.

Mineral soils are classified in a textural class based on the proportion of sand, silt, and clay. They, then, are named for the particles most responsible for the soil's characteristics. There are five major categories: coarse, moderately coarse, medium, moderately fine, and fine. The proportion of particles affects water retention and water availability. Generally, coarse soils such as sand or gravel have large air spaces that allow water to drain quickly; fine soils such as clay or silt have smaller pore spaces and, consequently, drain more slowly.

Texture also affects the soil's ability to retain nutrients for plant use. In a given volume of soil, there are more small particles than large ones. Therefore, the total particle surface of clay (top, bottom, and sides) is greater than sand. In other words, a handful of clay has more surface area than a handful of sand. Chemicals then bind to these particle surfaces—the greater the surface area, the more nutrient elements are available for plant use. Clay and silt have more surface area than sand or gravel and are, therefore, more fertile.

EXERCISE 3

Texture also determines the soil's workability. Smaller particles stick to each other more readily than larger ones. You will find that very gritty soil breaks apart easily as it is formed, whereas clay and silt hold together. For the landscape, a

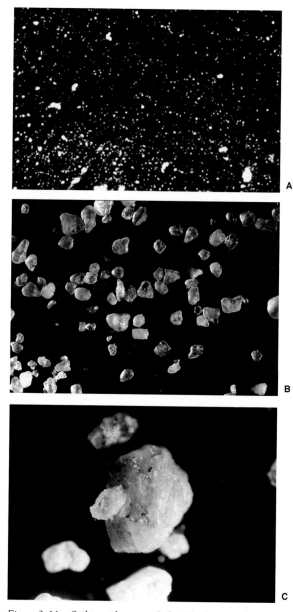

Figure 3.11—Soil particles magnified x 75: clay particles (slide A); fine sand particles (slide B); and coarse sand particles (slide C).

workable soil is one that holds together, but breaks apart when pressed. This type of soil is referred to as loam. Loam is a well-balanced mix of sand, silt, clay, and organic matter.

The following exercise is designed to help you determine how workable your soil is. Place $^1/_4$ cup of soil in the palm of your hand. Add water a few droplets at a time until the soil feels moist and holds together. If you have applied too much water, add more soil. As you add water, mold the soil into a ball, and answer the following questions starting with number one. Read both choices before moving to the next choice.

1a. Soil does not mold into a ball when squeezed. *If it does not, you have sand, go no further. If it does, go to 1b. (Sand is loose, single grained; individual grains are*

Figure 3.12—Sand, when squeezed, falls apart.

easily felt; if squeezed when dry, it falls apart; when moist, it molds, but crumbles under slight pressure (Figure 3.12).)

1b. Soil remains in a ball when squeezed *If yes, go to 2a. (Figure 3.13).*

2a. Soil falls apart when attempting to form into a long cigar shape. *If yes, you have loamy sand, go no further; if no, go to 2b.*
(Loamy sand, if carefully handled, has enough silt, and clay to hold its shape; there are many gradations of loam in which it can have 7 to 27 percent clay, 28 to 50 percent silt, and 50 percent sand.)

2b. Soil remains uniform in shape when worked into a long cigar shape. *If yes, go to 3a.*

Figure 3.13—Loamy sand remains in a ball.

3a. Soil makes a stubby cigar shape less than 1 inch long before breaking. *If yes, go to 4a; if no, skip down to 3b.*

3b. Soil makes a cigar shape larger than 2 inches before breaking, but is not very sticky. *If yes, go to 5a; if no, go to 3c.*

3c. Soil makes a strong cigar shape longer than 2 inches before breaking and is sticky. *If yes, go to 6a.*

Figure 3.14—Loam holds together (A) but breaks apart with some pressure (B).

4a. Soil feels gritty when rubbed between fingers. *If yes, you have sandy loam, go no further; if no, go to 4b.*

4b. Soil feels smooth. *If yes, you have silty loam, go no further; if no, go to 4c.*

4c. Soil feels neither predominately gritty nor smooth. *If yes, you have loam, go no further (Figure 3.14).*
(Loam has a slight gritty feel, but is somewhat smooth and slightly sticky. When dry, it forms a mold that holds together if handled carefully; if moist, it holds the mold with-out breaking apart easily. Silty loam may appear cloddy, but the clods are easily broken up when pressed.)

5a. Soil feels gritty. *If yes, you have sandy clay loam, go no further; if no, go to 5b.*

5b. Soil feels very smooth. *If yes, you have silty clay loam, go no further; if no, go to 5c.*

5c. Soil feels neither gritty, nor smooth, but slightly sticky. *If yes, you have a clay loam, go no further.*
(Clay loam breaks into clods that become hard as they dry; when moist, it molds into compact clumps that do not break apart readily.)

6a. Soil feels gritty and sticky. *If yes, you have sandy clay, if no, go to 6b.*

6b. Soil feels very smooth and sticky. *If yes, you have silty clay; if no, go to 6c.*

Figure 3.15—Clay soil makes cigar shape larger than 2 inches.

6c. Soil feels neither gritty nor smooth, but very sticky. *If yes, you have clay. (Figure 3.16).*

(Clay forms very hard clods when dry and is very sticky when wet; molds hold well; forms long, flat strips without breaking up. The longer and more adhesive the strip, the more clay the soil has; the more clay the soil has, the more difficult the soil is to work.) (Figures 15 & 16).

Figure 3.16—Clay is very sticky when wet.

SOIL TEXTURE AND XERISCAPE

Coarse texture

Plants need a balance of air and water for healthy growth and development. Soil provides both, though some does better than others. Coarse to moderately coarse soil such as rocky, sandy, gravelly soil, or loamy sand consist of larger particles that create large air spaces. Water drains quickly, leaving space for air. In a landscape, these soils need more frequent irrigation. A xeriscape landscape with such soils calls for plants that are more tolerant of dry soil conditions such as those native to deserts, semiarid grasslands, and shrub lands.

Medium Texture

Medium-textured soil or loam does a good job holding air, water, and nutrients because it consists of a balanced mix of sand, silt, clay, and organic matter. Most plants, whether from arid or humid environments, grow well in this type of soil although some plants from arid areas may become gangly with too much moisture (*Figure 3.17*). Medium-textured soils include sandy loam, loam, sandy clay loam, and silty loam. An all-purpose garden loam consists of 45 percent mineral particles (only 20 percent of mineral particles should be clay, otherwise, the soil is not easy to work), 5 percent organic matter, 25 percent water, and 25 percent air.

Fine texture

Fine-textured soil high in clay particles holds water tightly and does a poor job of providing oxygen. Plants that prefer moist soil can be grown under these conditions as long as irrigation is managed carefully and they are not overwatered. Dryland plants that normally grow in drier soil may rot if not carefully managed. Fine-textured soil includes clay, silty clay, sandy

loses its compact form.

Figure 3.18—Saturated soil.

clay, clay loam, and silty clay loam.

Very fine–textured soil with more than 40 percent clay feels gummy when wet and is difficult to manage. Wetland plants such as willows, alders, and cattails that are naturally found in low-lying areas and depressions where soil is saturated for periods of time are best suited to this type of soil (*Figure 3.18*).

Figure 3.19—Organic soil in a heath peat bog.

Organic soil

Soil that consists of organic matter extending at least 12 inches deep is considered organic and is described as muck, peat, and peaty muck. Plants associated with this type of soil are those that should be grown in cultivation when these conditions exist (*Figure 3.19*). Examples are heath and heather.

EXERCISE ON SOIL PROFILE

EXERCISE 4

This exercise examines the components of a soil profile, particularly layers A and B (topsoil and subsoil). With a spade, dig down 20 to 24 inches to see (a) how deep the top soil is; (b) if it is underlain by heavy clay, sand, or debris; and (c) if there is a compacted layer impeding drainage. Compacted soil is common in new developments or where heavy equipment has been used.

Review the entire profile you have exposed and look for changes in color. In layer A, lighter soils often indicate a coarse texture in which chemicals leach readily and temperatures are high. They may also indicate a lower level of organic material; otherwise, the surface will appear dark brown to black. The more organic matter there is, the darker the soil. Darker colors can also indicate poor drainage where temperatures and oxygen levels are low—possibly due to a high water table or hardpan. With fine-textured soil, if there are reds and yellows in layer A, it may merely indicate that some of the materials came from layer C. Mixed colors of reds and browns in layer B may mean that the parent material contains iron and it worked its way up into the above layer. In the subsoil, reds, browns, or a mix indicate the relatively easy movement of water. Gray or yellow in this layer generally indicates drainage problems (*Figure 3.20*).

Figure 3.20—Gray or yellow color in the soil profile may indicate drainage problems.

EXERCISE 5

Now, remove a slice of soil from the side wall and exert some slight pressure on it *(Figure 3.21)*. If the soil is easy to work, it will break into small crumbs when pressed and is considered friable or of good tilth. Soil that is hard and chunky is difficult to work and may stay wet for long periods of time.

Workable soil is determined, in part, by the soil structure or the way individual particles are held together into aggregates (or "peds"). Some types of aggregates are easier to work with than others. That is, soil may have "good" or "poor" structure. Soil with poor structure either won't hold together under pressure (sand) or forms clods that become very hard to break apart when dry (clay). Poor soil structure impedes drainage,

limiting areas conducive to active root development). For example, coarse sand exhibits poor structure because the individual particles are too large to hold together. Clay soil is prone to poor structure because its particles are so small they pack tightly together, filling every available space, which makes them difficult to separate. Loam has good structure and crumbles under slight pressure. Organic matter improves fine-textured soil, because through its decomposition the tiny clay particles become glued to larger ones. These, then, create bigger air spaces where water and air flow more freely, and plant roots move easily through these same channels *(Figure 3.23)*. Unless the soil is very coarse and not well developed, layer A of the soil profile generally has a workable (granular) structure because of its organic content. Good soil structure develops under grasses or sod because the fibrous roots, microorganisms, and dead organic material work together in creating particle aggregation. A workable garden soil should contain 3 to 5 percent organic material.

In layer B where the soil has more clay, aggregates tend to form smaller pore spaces between them. In part, this is due to a lack of sufficient organic materials, but it can also come about when the soil is worked while it is too wet or when the surface layer is removed either mechanically or by erosion.

Figure 3.21—Soil with good structure breaks with slight pressure.

Figure 3.22—Coarse sand particles too large to hold together.

Figure 3.23—Tiny clay particles form aggregates creating bigger air spaces.

SOIL NUTRIENTS AND pH

EXERCISE 6

Although nutrient elements exist in the soil, they may not necessarily be available to the plant. Their availability depends on whether they are soluble or insoluble and whether they can or cannot be released from the surface of the soil particle. Plant roots can only absorb what nutrients are available in soil moisture. Whether a nutrient is available or not depends on how acid or alkaline the soil is—the amount of hydrogen ions in the soil. Soil acidity can be diagnosed with a home soil-testing kit purchased at any garden center. The kit comes with an indicator dye solution and a color pH reading chart.

Acidity level is measured in pH units from 0 to 14 with 7 as neutral, above 7 alkaline, and below 7 acid. Because the units are exponential, a pH of 6 is 10 times more acidic than a pH of 7; a pH of 8 is 10 times more alkaline than a pH of 7.

Some plants grow in a restrictive pH range, but most plants in cultivation tolerate wider limits (*Figure 3.24*). Although soil pH can be ad-justed for the growing needs of specific plants, it is incompatible with xeriscape principles because soil adjustments require so much maintenance and resources. The more practical, conservative approach is to select plants that will thrive in the existing pH.

Climate has a direct effect on soil pH. Humid areas with more precipitation tend to develop thicker layers of topsoil in a shorter period of time. As organic matter accumulates and decomposes, the soil tends to become more acidic. The southeastern United States is home to many azaleas, rhododendrons, and laurels that thrive in a pH of 5.5. In drier, more arid regions with less precipitation and higher solar radiation, organic material is slower to build up, salts are not leached (washed out), and the soil becomes more alkaline. The Southwest is home to sagebrush, rabbitbrush, and juniper in soil where the pH is around 8.0. In urban areas, soil is variable, but the weathering of concrete and asphalt along with alkaline irrigation water add to its alkalinity.

NUTRIENTS AND FERTILIZERS

Good plant nutrition is essential for healthy plants. The soil's ability to supply needed nutritional elements can be (if necessary) improved with fertilizers (see Chapter IV on fertilizers). Presently, eighteen nutrient elements have been identified as necessary for plant growth. Two of them (carbon from carbon dioxide and oxygen) come from air or are dissolved in water. Nitrogen comes from the atmosphere, but has to be incorporated into more complex chemicals for it to be available for plant use. The remaining nutrients are derived from the soil. Some nutrients (carbon, oxygen, nitrogen, potassium, phosphorus, calcium, magnesium, and sulfur are consumed in larger amounts than others, such as iron, manganese, copper, zinc, boron, molybdenum, chlorine, sodium, and cobalt. The

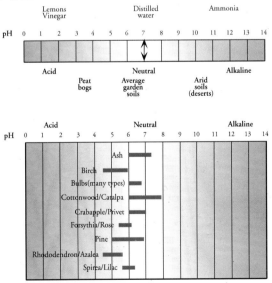

Figure 3.24—Most plants tolerate a wide pH range.

latter are referred to as micronutrients because they are needed in such small quantities. Nonetheless, all nutrients contribute to a plant's overall good health. In a natural, undisturbed ecosystem, nutrient elements are continuously being used and returned to the soil and air through decomposition and recycling *(Figure. 3.25)*. In a cultivated landscape, they are often removed by traditional maintenance and clean-up practices. Potential recyclable nutrition for plants originates in leaves, flowers, and fruits. Often, in ignorance, these are bagged and buried in landfills and then (the freely given elements that we throw out) are replaced with fertilizers we buy from a garden center or hardware store.

Figure 3.25—Nutrients being returned to the soil through decomposition and recycling.

PROFESSIONAL SOIL TESTS

For a professional soil analysis, you can send soil samples to your county cooperative extension service or a private laboratory. Soil tests identify pH, provide information regarding texture, water-holding qualities, available nutrient elements, and salt content. For specific plants or crops, they also provide guidelines on fertilizer and soil amendments. The soil sample should be a composite of random samples taken throughout the area of concern at a depth of 2 to 8 inches where the majority of plant roots do or will exist. Soil-testing laboratories provide complete instructions.

EXERCISE ON SOIL DRAINAGE

EXERCISE 7

Soil that stores moisture yet drains well is one of the best contributors to healthy, vigorous plants. Soil drainage is the rate and extent at which water moves through the profile. Good drainage is essential to maintaining pore space for air. Although plants must have water for photosynthesis and numerous other processes, they need oxygen as well. Roots extract oxygen from the air in the soil and transport it to cells, where it then combines with other molecules. It is subsequently returned to the air either in the soil or in the atmosphere as carbon dioxide.

This exercise will help you determine how well your soil drains. Dig a hole 12 inches deep and fill it with water. Test each area where soil differs. After one hour, measure the depth of water in the hole. Soil in which water moves 1 inch or more per hour is fast draining. If this is the case, cultivate plants that tolerate dry soil. Less than $1/4$ inch per hour indicates slow drainage. Consider growing plants from wetland areas. Water that drains between $1/4$ to 1 inch per hour indicates soil drainage characteristics that

Figure 3.26—One half cup water in sand (A) and one half cup water in clay (B).

are desirable for most plants. If, after twenty-four hours, standing water remains, you might consider planting elsewhere or design for a bog or pond environment.

There are ways to improve drainage mechanically, by breaking through hardpans or using drain tiles or raised beds. Very poor drainage can be caused by a number of variables: compacted soil, hardpan, water leaks, and a high water table. You may want to seek the advice of an engineer or landscape architect.

Clay holds more water than sand; therefore, it takes more water to wet at a given depth than sand. One inch of water wets clay soil 4 inches deep, sandy soil 12 inches deep, and a sandy loam 6 inches deep (*Figure 3.26*).

Another impact of soil texture on water infiltration and drainage is that it causes water to move through adjacent soil layers of different textures. If you place fine-textured soil on top of coarse-textured soil in a planting hole, water will saturate the tighter soil first before it moves through the coarser one. Thus, gravel or sand at the bottom of a planting hole does not improve drainage. In addition, when you place a container plant that's growing in looser soil than the landscape soil, water will move toward the tighter (finer) soil and away from the loose, coarser one. Months later, the plant may show signs of stress because the soil ball is dry, even though the adjacent soil is moist.

Soil Water

Periodically, when there is a drought, we become concerned about water and, for a short time, realize how precious and threatened this resource is. Once the drought passes, however, we tend to forget.

Plants need water because it is a critical element to all their life processes. During a plant's active growth stage, more than 90 percent of its structure is composed of water. Water transports nutrients, is a main ingredient in photosynthesis, is essential to hormone and enzyme synthesis, and affects the size and length of stem, root, leaf, and fruit. When water enters the soil, it moves downward through the various soil layers. The first layer is where most of the fine roots and root hairs are and is usually higher in organic matter, oxygen, and microorganisms. If there is sufficient water and adequate drainage, water then moves from layer A to the next layer, carrying unused nutrient elements with it until it ultimately reaches a saturated zone (the water table). If the amount of water is insufficient to move through the soil profile, it moves as far as it can. Nutrients and salts that are not passed on through the

Figure 3.27—Evaporation may leave salts behind on the soil surface.

soil (leached) may accumulate, potentially forming an impermeable base. They may even move up to the surface through capillary action (interaction between soil and water due to cohesive and adhesive properties). Once it reaches the surface, the water evaporates and leaves the salts behind. This is a common occurrence in arid regions. High levels of salts may damage plant growth, unless the plants have evolved mechanisms to deal with these conditions (*Figure 3.27*).

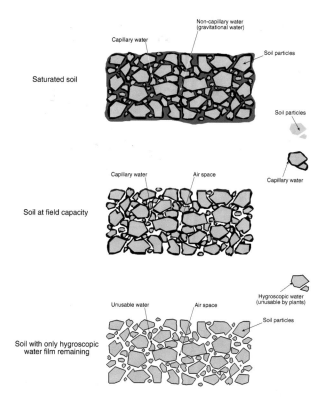

Figure 3.28—Types of soil water.

Figure 3.29—Signs of initial wilt.

use. Capillary water (held in the soil because the surface tension around the soil particles is stronger than gravity) stays. At this time, spaces where gravitational water used to be fill with air and the soil is no longer saturated, but at "field capacity." Capillary water is available for plant use and the soil is in an optimum condition for growing plants because both air and water are available at the same time. Field capacity, however, soon changes as plants begin to use the water, or it evaporates through the surface and the soil begins to dry out. The drier it gets, the tighter the remaining water is held to each particle and the more difficult it becomes for the plants to extract. Eventually, there is no more capillary water. The only moisture that remains is a thin hygroscopic water film tightly bound to the soil particle. This is not available to plants because it takes too much energy to remove it from the soil particle surface. If soil moisture reaches this point and is not replaced, the plant may suffer a water deficit.

While all plants need water, some tolerate water deficits better than others. Wilt is often the first symptom, especially in broadleaf deciduous plants. Such plants can recover from an initial wilt, but if water is not replenished over a long period of time, the plants will die (Figure 3.29).

To visualize water moving through soil, imagine the droplets as they enter. They silently flow through the profile from top to bottom, touching and surrounding each soil particle, filling each small, open space. Some water stays around (capillary water), other water escapes (gravitational water) through the forces of gravity. If both gravitational and capillary water leave the soil, a third type called "hygroscopic" water still remains (Figure 3.28).

If soil contains all of these water types, soil conditions are saturated. This usually occurs after a thorough irrigation or lengthy rain. Depending on the soil, gravitational water that occupied the large spaces soon drains away. Because it is so transient, it is not available for plants to

SOIL, WATER, AND PLANTS IN THE LANDSCAPE

Most plants commonly used in the cultivated landscape grow naturally in humid environ-

ments such as moist forests, where soil capillary pores are generally supplied with sufficient water on a regular basis. These plants usually lack the ability to tolerate dry soil for any length of time and in the landscape may require frequent irrigation, especially when cultivated in more arid regions. Plants from more arid and semiarid environments, on the other hand, have a greater ability to thrive and tolerate dry soil without wilting. Their water stress may be expressed as unseasonable dormancy, leaf drop, shrinkage of tissue, leaves rolling inward, loss of color, or retraction into the soil (*Figure 3.30*). The time it takes for plant wilt to cause permanent plant damage depends on the soil and plant being grown.

Figure 3.30—Plant adaptation to water deficit.

SOIL FOR HEALTHY PLANT GROWTH

The ideal all-around landscape soil should: a) allow easy penetration of water, air, and roots; b) retain water between rains or irrigation and allow the excess to drain; and c) have a balanced supply of available nutrients. Loam is the most versatile soil and would meet all of these needs, but it is also the least common. However, soil can be improved by adding materials appropriate to the existing conditions and the plants being grown. Unfortunately, this is not a quick, easy solution because it takes numerous growing seasons to improve the soil, and, in some cases, the area may be too large to make it either economical or practical. Before making any decisions about amending soil, ask yourself the following questions:

1) What is the desired soil condition?
2) What is needed for the soil to attain that desired condition?
3) Is the area large and, thus, how practical is it to improve the soil?
4) Will it do any good?
5) Are there any other options?

The goal in improving soil is to create an environment in which roots are allowed to absorb water, nutrients, and air in order to support healthy plants. How you get there may take many paths. Evaluate them all before proceeding.

PATHS TO SOIL IMPROVEMENT
- Improve soil by adding amendments
- Grow cover crops or green manure
- Aerate the soil
- Select plants best suited to existing soil
- Manage the soil carefully
- Preserve and protect the soil

IMPROVING SOIL BY ADDING AMENDMENTS

Amendments are used to improve soil aeration and the drainage of fine-textured or compacted soil, or they are used to increase the water- and nutrient-holding capacities of coarse soil. They are not fertilizers, although some may contribute small amounts of nutrients to the soil. Conversely, fertilizers are not amendments. They supplement the soil's supply of nutrient elements (see Chapter IV on fertilizer).

FINE -TEXTURED SOIL
Clay is one of the more difficult landscape soils to work with because it has small pore spaces and drains slowly. One way to improve it is to add organic matter. Through the process of decomposition, organic matter facilitates the granulation of the fine clay particles that in turn create larger pore spaces, resulting in soil that is easier to work.

Figure 3.31—Compaction impedes soil drainage.

Any time you work with clay soil, because it is prone to compaction and poor structure, timing is critical. Potential damage can be lessened by minimizing tillage, using a spading fork, and handling the soil when moisture levels are ideal. Working clay when it is too wet compresses the tiny particles together, collapsing the air spaces in between. Compaction in the topsoil kills many of the microorganisms and leads to the formation of a surface crust, thus inhibiting water penetration *(Figure 3.31)*. Rain and irrigation contribute to crusting by forcing the tiny particles into the pore spaces. As a result, puddling or standing water may occur on top, even though it is dry underneath. Compaction that occurs below the top layer creates hardpans that also impede drainage. You can gauge the moisture level by squeezing a handful of soil. If it stays in a mass, it is too wet; if it crumbles under pressure it is ready to work.

Other than adding organic matter to improve air/water ratios in clay soil, coarse sand can also be added. Its disadvantage is the amount needed—at least 40 to 50 percent by volume; otherwise, clay and sand fill all the small spaces and the soil behaves like concrete.

COARSE-TEXTURED SOIL

Coarse, sandy to gravelly soils are the antithesis of clay. They are easier to work wet or dry, but they drain quickly and hold few nutrients. In order to increase their water and nutrient retention, corrective treatment also entails adding organic matter because of its retentive qualities. Materials should be incorporated thoroughly. If organic matter is fresh, additional nitrogen fertilizer is recommended because both the microorganisms in the newly added organic material and young plants are competing for the same supply of nitrogen. If organic matter is thoroughly composted or aged, supplemental fertilizer is not needed.

ORGANIC AMENDMENTS

Organic matter used as an amendment should have two characteristics: it should be a renewable resource and it should be safe. Peat, mountain peat, and sphagnum peat are not renewable resources when removed from their natural ecosystems. To extract these materials, natural areas are mined and wetlands are drained. A most appropriate amendment is recycled compost (see Chapter IV on compost). **Compost** is safe and inexpensive, especially if you create your own. It is useful in both sandy and clay soils and makes use of materials that otherwise end up in landfills. **Manure** is a commonly used amendment because it is inexpensive and widely available. It varies in quality depending on the source of the animal's diet—weed seeds can be a problem. Too much organic matter added at one time may increase natural soluble salts in the amended layer and too fresh a material can create a temporary nitrogen deficiency. For semiarid and arid areas with saline soil, materials high in salts such as sludge or manure should be avoided as they will only compound the salt problem. Organic matter is considered safe and ready to use as an amendment when it is partially decomposed, odorless, and crumbles when touched. If using manure, well-rotted, aged manure can be incorporated into the soil at least two weeks before planting. To be safe, fresh manure should sit two to three months, or if incorporated, the area should not be planted for two to three months.

Recommended application rates for organic matter are 1 inch of amendment for every 4 inches of soil being amended or 3 cubic yards per 1,000 square feet. Incorporate and mix as thoroughly and as deeply as possible. Safe soil improvement should be an ongoing process that continues over a period of years.

INORGANIC AMENDMENTS

Inorganic materials are inert amendments that produce minimal chemical reactions. When they are added to the soil, depending on the amount, they may change soil texture and, as a result, improve soil drainage. Sand, vermiculite, turface, or perlite are examples. Of the inert materials, sand is the most commonly used for tight, fine-textured soil. Other materials are not as adaptable especially for large areas. Adding sand to clay requires at least 40 to 50 percent by volume.

To retain moisture in sandy soil, perlite and vermiculite have been used. Perlite is a heat-expanded volcanic glass that retains moisture; vermiculite is a heat-expanded material derived from mica. Both are more commonly used in soil mixes for container plants or for starting cuttings and seedlings. New materials in the marketplace are the "hydrogels." These are gel-like particles that absorb hundreds of times their weight in water. Their use may be appropriate for container plants or sandy soil. Their use in large field plantings is still in question (*Figure 3.32*).

THE PRACTICALITY OF AMENDING SOIL

Amending soil is an ongoing process and is recommended in areas where high yields are expected (such as vegetable gardens) and where plants are removed annually (annual, vegetable, and perennial flower displays). Amendments are also desirable when preparing a bed of manageable size along borders or small island plantings of small trees and shrubs. They can be added slowly each year as you work and mulch the soil. Developing a good garden loam by adding organic matter is a slow process demanding patience and repetition. The amended soil area should be of sufficient size both in depth and width for existing roots

Figure 3.32—Hydrogels absorb water (left) many times their weight.

and expected root growth. In areas where plant roots will be shallow and dense, soil should be amended at least 6 to 8 inches deep; for deeper rooted plants such as trees, shrubs, and grasses, soil should be amended at least 8 to 12 inches; 18 inches is preferable.

Amending soil in a confined space or for special crops is feasible, but how do you deal with an entire landscape? What will it take, what are the costs and what are the benefits? The decision to improve soil in a large area should be based on economics, time, and whether it will make a difference. When planting trees or shrubs, you need to ascertain how much area to amend since roots will ultimately grow beyond the planting hole. Knowing it takes years to modify soil, is it of any benefit to amend soil on a one-time basis when planting permanent plants? To have an impact on soil characteristics in a short period of time, it takes a lot of material. When adding sand to clay soil, 40 to 50 percent of the existing clay soil needs to be removed and replaced with equal amounts of sand. To change sandy soil to loam, 30 to 40 percent of the existing soil needs to be removed and replaced with equal amounts of organic matter. Too much organic matter added at one time increases soluble salts and is potentially harmful to plants.

IMPROVING SOIL WITH COVER CROPS OR GREEN MANURE

Another approach to safe soil amendment is planting a cover crop or "green manure." Green manure is a temporary cover crop grown for a short period of time and then turned into the soil to decompose. Species used as cover crops are herbaceous plants that grow quickly in part of one season. For example, seeds can be sown in late fall and turned over in early spring. After about two weeks, the soil is ready to plant. Using a cover crop for vegetable gardens and turf grass areas prior to planting has dual benefits. Not only does it improve the soil for planting, but it also protects it from erosion. Winter rye, winter wheat, barley, and buckwheat are commonly used. For more information on cover crops, check with your local cooperative extension or the natural resource conservation service *(Figure 3.33)*.

Figure 3.33—Cover crops provide temporary soil cover and protection.

Improving Soil by Aeration

If soil is compacted or exhibits poor air movement, the soil may not need amending, it may need the compacted layer broken up or it may need to be aerated. The latter is achieved by breaking up hardpans and soil clods or by coring. Aeration introduces air into compacted or tight soil by poking holes several inches into it or removing soil cores. Once the cores are removed, they can be broken up and replaced or left on the surface to decompose *(Figure 3.34)*. Another technique is to drill holes in the existing soil and fill them with organic matter or looser soil.

Figure 3.34—Removing soil cores is one way to improve soil aeration.

Other areas where amendments may not help are soils with expansive clay (swells when wet and shrinks/cracks when dry). These soils are commonly found in semiarid grassland regions and can present problems if amended with organic matter and then irrigated. When they expand and shrink, they may cause mud slides or may crack foundations. With these soils, hand spade the area to aerate the soil for root penetration (this may need to be done several times) and break up any hardpans. Do not allow the soil to swing from wet to dry and plant vegeta-

Figure 3.35—Expansive clay swells when wet and shrinks when dry.

tion that is indigenous to this soil type (short-grass prairie) *(Figure 3.35)*.

Selecting Plants Best Suited to the Existing Soil

It is more practical, less frustrating, and often less expensive to select the appropriate plant for the site rather than changing the site for the plant. For example, if the soil has a pH of 8.0 (alkaline), do not plant materials that require a pH of 6.0. Appropriate plant selection means choosing plants that will best tolerate the existing site.

CAREFUL SOIL MANAGEMENT

Careful management is another way to deal with difficult soil conditions. For example, monitoring irrigation and using fertilizers and mulch efficiently may be the most practical ways of dealing with coarse soil in which plants need frequent irrigation. Rather than adding materials to the soil to retain more moisture, it may be more sensible to use drip irrigation and mulch to reduce evaporation and keep the soil cooler. Slow-release fertilizers can provide addition nutrients (see Chapter IV on mulch and fertilizers).

PRESERVING AND PROTECTING THE SOIL

If you are building on a new site and your property is partially undisturbed land, plan ahead to protect this valuable resource. You can get a USDA soil conservation map identifying the soil type, its properties, and its characteristics. Work with your contractor to avoid potential damage. Are there any areas where the soil can be left undisturbed? Can it be protected to avoid damage? Is there any natural vegetation and can it remain? Ideally, it is always less costly, less time-consuming and less frustrating to leave the soil undisturbed and potentially unchanged, especially where there are existing plants or where plants are going to be. In this area, leaf litter can accu-

Figure 3.36—Plan ahead to protect valuable natural resources such as soil and native plant communities.

mulate and decompose providing a natural mulch and compost, and microorganisms can remain undisturbed (*Figure 3.36*).

CHAPTER IV

Compost, Mulch, and Fertilizer

Compost

Composting is essentially a recycling process whereby microorganisms break down organic materials into basic elements which are then returned to the soil to be used again. In nature, if materials weren't recycled, dead organisms would accumulate and the natural ecosystems would eventually run out of nutrients to continue life. It makes sense to conserve resources in the landscape rather than disturbing natural environments to extract them (mining peat moss from wetlands) or to reuse kitchen and yard wastes instead of sending them to landfills. We can do this by composting *(Figure 4.1)*.

In a xeriscape, composting plays an integral role in conservation. Compost can be used as a soil amendment or mulch, as well as provide some nutrients for plant growth. Because it is organic, as an amendment it improves soil aera-tion in heavy clay and water and improves nutrient retention in sand. It can also be used as part of a soil mix for container plants. Some gardeners put compost in a burlap pouch, let it steep in water, and use it as a liquid fertilizer ("green tea").

Figure 4.1— Composting—reusing kitchen and garden wastes.

HOW COMPOSTING WORKS

The easiest way to see compost in process is in a natural forest. If you look at the forest floor, natural composting starts with leaf litter, twigs, animal feces, and other nonliving organic debris that accumulate on the ground. On the surface, the litter and its composition are fairly easy to identify, but as you dig deeper, you will notice how pieces become progressively smaller and less identifiable. Ultimately they become part of a fluffy, dark mass called "humus." When rain or snow falls, some of the humus moves deeper into the soil and some of the elements go into solution that can be absorbed by plant roots *(Figure 4.2)*.

Composting takes place in all natural ecosystems—some are slower than others because of differences in temperature, moisture, and air (e.g., forest decomposition is faster than desert decomposition). For soil organisms, composting creates a hierarchy of who eats and who gets eaten. That is, when organic material is broken

Figure 4.2—From plant litter (A) to humus (B).

down, small animals and microorganisms act in sequence as they digest and decompose twigs, leaves, and skeletons, until the organic material is reduced to its basic elements. These elements and minute particles beneficially alter soil properties and supply chemical nutrients for plant growth. Of particular importance is the supply of fixed nitrogen (see fertilizer section) that becomes available in a form plants can use.

It's easy to make composting a routine part of gardening and landscape maintenance. Recycling materials can be done by design. Simply allow leaf litter to remain in place once it falls. Soil organisms will take care of the rest. This approach works well when trees are planted in groups rather than as specimens. Grass clippings that are left on the lawn represent another single way of composting. Or you can allocate space for a compost pile—at least 3 cubic feet for the pile with some elbow room to work in. If possible, the compost pile should be located where it is convenient to transport kitchen and yard wastes. It functions best in partial shade where it can be protected from drying out too rapidly and near a hose or sprinkler to keep it moist. Aesthetically, it can be screened with plantings or enclosed in an attractively designed structure.

Various ready-to-use structures are available commercially, or you can create a free-standing pile. What you choose mostly depends on time, space, purpose, and cost. Even among the ready-made structures, there are ways to modify them. Some manufactured compost bins and storage equipment are expensive. It is just as easy to keep it simple and cheap. Free-standing piles with no enclosure, compost space surrounded by chicken wire, wooden pallets, and metal or plastic tumblers (rotating barrels) are some possibilities (*Figure 4.3*).

How to Compost

The important factors in successful composting are temperature, moisture, air circulation, and food (kitchen and yard wastes) for the organisms that labor to decompose the organic matter. These all work in concert to determine how quickly the pile breaks down.

TEMPERATURE
Decomposition can occur anywhere between 0 and 200°F; however, most decomposing organisms are active in the range of 70 to 140°F. A well-managed compost breaks down quickly when the interior temperature ranges between 120 to 130°F. The center is usually hottest because the ongoing metabolic processes produce heat and the center is more insulated.

MOISTURE AND AIR
Moisture is crucial to compost because microorganisms need it for digestion. A dry compost slows the process down. Ideally, the pile should have the consistency of a damp sponge. If it's too

wet, air cannot circulate through the pile and anaerobic microorganisms (those acting in the absence of oxygen) can take over. These generate offensive odors and are less efficient. Good air circulation can be facilitated by using different sizes of particles and turning the compost pile often. Larger particles enable air to move more freely, and they also prevent matting.

INGREDIENTS

Food we provide for the microorganisms (material to be composted) comes from our yard and kitchen wastes. A balance of 30 parts carbon to 1 part nitrogen is ideal. Carbon is necessary for energy and nitrogen is essential for protein to keep the composting organisms going. Woody and dried plant materials from yard wastes are high in carbon; fresh green materials such as grass clippings and weeds or fresh trimmings are high in nitrogen.

Yard wastes include leaves, stems, twigs, flowers, vegetables, and fruits. Kitchen wastes include fruits, vegetable peelings, apple cores, banana peels, coffee grounds, eggshells, and carrot peelings, among others. You can also use old potting soil, shredded black and white newspapers, animal fur, dryer lint, and vacuum cleaner debris. Newspapers should make up no more than 10 percent of the total weight of the composted material. You'll find that some plants (pines, junipers, and arborvitae) take longer to break down because of their resin. These can be composted separately. Others high in tannin, such as oaks and cottonwood, can be mixed with different material or shredded to speed up their decomposition. Animal products that can be composted include bone meal and manure from plant-eating animals such as cows, sheep, rabbits, and chickens. However, avoid other animal and dairy products such as bones, grease, or

Two-bin composter made with wooden slats

Figure 4.3—Various composting structures (counter clockwise from top left) (A) free-form; (B) wood and wire; (C) cement block; (D) tumbler; (E) garden gourmet; (F) soil maker; and (G) wood slats drawing.

whole eggs as they cause odors that can attract rodents and other pests. Avoid cat, dog, or other domestic pet feces as they may carry disease. If the compost is to be used as a soil amendment, you may want to test the pH periodically. Some materials such as wood ash are alkaline and others like pine and oak leaves are acidic.

Diseased plants or weeds that have gone to seed should not go in the compost pile, especially if it doesn't get hot enough. If the pile doesn't get above 90°F, the seeds and pathogens may remain viable. When compost is used as an amendment or mulch, the seeds and pathogens are then spread, creating a weed or maintenance problem.

Ideally, compost begins with alternating layers of organic materials of different-size particles until there is a manageable pile. The pile is then turned at least once or twice a month. (Ideally, it should be turned when internal temperatures reach between 120 to 160°F and then drop). To turn the compost, rotate outside materials to the bottom and interior materials to the outside. Once composting is complete, the mass will be much smaller than its original size and will exude an earthy smell (*Figure 4.4*).

It takes anywhere from three weeks to two years to transform raw material to humus. The amount of time depends on environmental conditions, size and types of materials, and the methods used. Passive piles of compost take longer because there is little activity, such as turning them and keeping them moist to speed up the

Layer 1— open ground

Layer 2— 4 to 6 inches of woody and dried materials no larger than 1 to 2 inches in diameter

Layer 3— approximately 1 inch of compost, leaf mold, or soil

Layer 4— green material and kitchen wastes

Figure 4.4—Layering organic material into a manageable pile.

process. The ultimate passive compost is merely storing compostable materials and allowing them to slowly decompose. Passive compost heaps can take several years, plus they also take up space. To speed the process, materials can be shredded or chopped into small pieces. There are shredders that cut up leaves that can reduce approximately four to eight garbage bags of leaves to just one. The shredded leaves can then be placed in the compost pile. Chippers and shredders also break woody material into smaller pieces. Nonwoody and small pieces are fed through the top of the machine and larger wood trimmings go through a side chute (*Figure 4.5*).

Figure 4.5—Shredders break materials into smaller pieces.

OTHER METHODS OF COMPOSTING

Other ways to compost involve using a green cover crop or green manure (see Chapter III on amendments) and mulch composting to improve soil, soil fertility, and prevent erosion. For a cover crop, a plant such as annual rye grain is sown on bare soil. Before it gets too tall or matures and goes to seed, it is either mowed down or it is turned under to decompose in place. If mowed, this process continues until the plant dies because of cold temperatures or until the crop is turned into the soil. If the crop dies and is not turned under, the area can be drill seeded, keeping the organic material in place.

Mulch composting means spreading dried, shredded material over the top of the soil. It slowly breaks down and very gradually filters into the soil. To maintain an organic mulch at the surface it needs to be replenished as it decomposes or it can be tilled under as with green manure. Leaving grass clippings on the lawn after mowing is an example of mulch composting. There are mulching mowers that chop lawn clippings, spew them out, and blow them back onto the turf where they decompose and replenish nutrients. Research indicates that regular mowing when the grass is $1^1/_2$ inches tall without removing clippings will provide all the nitrogen the lawn needs. Think of the time, energy, and money saved in raking, bagging, and fertilizing, not to mention the space saved in landfills (Figure 4.6).

Figure 4.6—Mulching mowers chop lawn clippings and blow them onto the turf.

Mulch

Mulch in the natural environment consists of leaf litter, dead grass blades, twigs, pieces of bark, and insect skeletons, to name a few. In the forest, it is a dominant feature year-round. On the prairie, it is most obvious in winter when grass blades are flattened against the soil (Figure 4.7).

Mulching, like composting, can be adapted to the cultivated landscape not only to reuse resources, but to help protect what is already there. In cultivation, mulching lessens weed competition, reduces the frequency of irrigation, and minimizes winter damage from freezing and thawing (that heaves plants out of the ground). It reduces the need for cultivation and as a result there is less damage to roots and less disturbance of the soil structure and soil organisms. As a design element, decorative mulch can unify a landscape plan and give a newly planted area a finished look. As a protection for soil, mulch moderates soil temperatures and safeguards it from erosion, compaction, crusting, and excessive evaporation. It provides shelter and habitats for many important microorganisms. In some cases, as it decomposes, organic mulch also supplies nutrient elements for plant use.

As many benefits as mulch provides, there are times when the wrong choice of material can adversely affect plant growth. Organic mulch around dryland plants with numerous hairs and succulent stems may keep the environment too moist and cause the crowns to rot, or it may keep the soil too moist and cool, causing roots to rot (Figure 4.8). Likewise, stones or gravel around plants with large, thin leaves raise

Figure 4.7—Forest mulch consists mostly of tree leaves, prairie mulch consists mostly of grass blades.

Figure 4.8—Organic mulch surrounding dryland plants may cause them to rot.

air temperatures, increasing transpiration and potentially scorching the leaves. Young tissue growth and plants that are not well established are particularly susceptible.

TYPES OF MULCH

In a broad sense, mulch can be anything that covers the soil, including ground cover plants. However, in general, mulch is divided into two main categories: organic mulches are natural plant products; inorganic materials are stone, rock, earthenware, and synthetic products.

ORGANIC MULCH

Organic mulches—fresh or dried, herbaceous or woody—are derived from plants and their by-products. They weather and decompose with time and, if not removed, recycle back into the landscape. Nonwoody organic mulches break down quickly and are best used with seasonal plantings or as a temporary cover. Straw, grass clippings, pine needles, and hay are some examples. Other nonwoody, organic materials that may be used as a mulch, but are more frequently applied as a soil amendment, include compost, manure, and leaf mold.

Woody materials such as chipped or shredded wood and bark last one to several years, depending on the type and size. The larger the pieces, the longer it takes to break down. If a woody mulch is replenished from time to time, it can be relatively permanent. Choices of mulch may depend on what is available in your area.

Organic mulches differ in texture, chemical properties, and their workability. Some are more difficult to put down than others (*Figure 4.9*).

INORGANIC MULCH

Inorganic mulches consist of either synthetic fabrics such as plastics or geotextiles, or are

Figure 4.9—Organic materials used as a mulch: (A) pine needles; (B) pine cones; (C) small bark nuggets; (D) shredded wood mix; (E) wood peelings.

Figure 4.10—Inorganic mineral mulch: (A) pea gravel; (B) scoria; (C) river rock; (D) volcanic rock; (E) granite; (F) rocks used in a dry stream.

inert, natural materials such as rock, gravel, or sand. Unlike organic mulches, they cannot be incorporated in the soil nor do they add any measurable nutrients. To eliminate them from the landscape, they have to be physically removed.

Natural inorganic mulches of rocks, gravel, sand, and other mineral products last a long time. Their textures vary with mining and manufacturing processes and their design appeal is associated with dry streams, rock gardens, desert or dryland landscapes, and water gardens *(Figure 4.10)*. As a mulch, their effectiveness is sometimes compromised by weed seeds that blow in and are difficult to remove and by heat reflection that raises air temperatures 10 to 30°F. Some minerals may also alter the soil pH.

Plastic mulches warm the soil and are frequently used to extend the plants' growing season, especially vegetables. Although it is relatively inexpensive, it deteriorates with exposure to temperature, sun, and chemicals, breaks down slowly in a landfill, reduces the air exchange between the atmosphere and soil, and is unattractive and slippery.

Synthetic fabrics or geotextiles used as weed barriers are composed of fibers from petroleum by-products. Each type of fabric varies in strength, composition, stability, and function. Porous landscape fabrics are more effective weed barriers than solid black plastic because they at least allow water and air to reach plant roots. They are also easier to cut and form to the ground. All fabric manufacturers recommend covering the fabrics with additional mulch, such as rock or wood chips, since sunlight breaks the fibers down, plus, they are not particularly attractive. If

Figure 4.11—Synthetic fabric used as a weed barrier.

you are considering using these products, look at the manufacturing and bonding processes, composition, color, weight, thickness, puncture and tear strength, water and air flow, expense, and how and with what you will cover them (*Figure 4.11*).

SELECTING A MULCH

Select a mulch to fit your design style and complement the environment. Determine how you want to use it, when and how it is to be applied, and what plants (if any) it will protect. Ideally, a mulch should last a long time, be easy to apply, inexpensive, locally available, aesthetically pleasing, and compatible with the plants it surrounds. Plants from semiarid to arid areas that naturally grow in dry soils combine well with mineral products of sand, crushed stone, or crushed earthenware, as well as low-growing, short, warm-season grasses such as blue grama grass intermixed with wildflowers (*Figure 4.12*). A dryland landscape of this nature has a different look, a different feel, and invites a soil cover other than wood products. Plants naturally found in moist soil and humid environments combine well with organic mulches of wood chips, bark, leaf litter, or green ground covers.

In a conventional landscape with trees as specimens and lawn as a ground cover, the natural mulch is often removed. Leaf litter and grass clippings are raked in piles, loaded in plastic bags, and taken to landfills. In a xeriscape landscape designed for lower maintenance and conservation of resources, mulching as a natural ecological process is more likely to occur when trees are grouped in groves and where leaf litter is allowed to fall and collect. The soil is neither tilled nor cultivated (other than some hand weeding). An appropriate vegetative cover might consist of upright, loosely formed plants that are 12 inches high and that will allow litter to fall through to the soil surface.

When plants are used as a ground cover and mulch, they should be tall enough to inhibit weeds from emerging from the soil surface, dense enough to prevent blown-in seeds from making

Figure 4.12—Cactus combines with stone mulch.

Figure 4.13—Creeping hollygrape (Mahonia repens), an attractive year-round ground cover.

soil contact and germinating, fast enough to cover the area within one to two years, tough enough to take some foot traffic, and be attractive and low maintenance as well (*Figure 4.13*).

In semiarid and arid regions, be alert to the fire potential of some materials. Those most susceptible dry out quickly, and include cornstalks, grass clippings, paper, and pine needles. If these are being used, they may need to be moistened when dry conditions exist.

WHEN TO APPLY MULCH

You can apply mulch at any time of the year. In spring, it dresses up newly planted areas, giving them a more finished look. In summer it can be used in flower and vegetable gardens to reduce evaporation and protect plant roots from the hot sun. In fall, it can be applied while the soil is still warm, providing a longer period conducive to root growth. In winter it can be applied when the ground is frozen, although it may potentially delay the emergence of early spring plants such as tulips. In winter, because there can be as much as 10 to 25°F temperature difference between the soil and air, mulch keeps the soil warmer and provides additional insulation from the cold. Additionally, mulch placed after a hard frost may keep the soil frozen, lessening the freeze/thaw action that causes shallow-rooted plants to heave and dry out.

HOW MUCH MULCH?

How much mulch is needed depends on what you use. If the product is very fine, 2 inches may be adequate. However, fine-textured mulch has the potential of packing together, inhibiting water penetration. If the material is very coarse such as bark nuggets, 4 inches should be used. For medium-textured materials such as wood chips and shredded bark, mulch should be applied at least 3 inches thick. The objective is to apply a mulch thick enough to prevent blown-in weed seeds from getting established in the soil or encouraging seeds already in the soil to run out of stored energy before they can surface

TABLE 4.1: TYPES OF MULCH		
coarse texture	**medium texture**	**fine texture**
bark chunks	landscape fabric	compost
cornstalks	leaf mold/leaves	crushed stone
gravel	pine needles	grass clippings
marble	pine/spruce cones	manure
stone	shavings	pea gravel
	shredded bark/wood	sand
	stone	sawdust
	straw	
temporary mulch	**wind-resistant mulch**	
compost	bark/wood chips/chunks	
evergreen boughs	compost	
grass clippings	evergreen boughs	
leaf mold	gravel	
manure	leaves (partially decomposed	
sawdust	and packed)	
shavings	manure	
straw	pine/spruce cones	
waste paper	pine needles	
	shredded bark/wood	
	stone	

and photosynthesize. Too much organic mulch, on the other hand, can be undesirable, causing roots to develop in the mulch layer and not the soil. When applying the material around trees and shrubs, leave several inches of space at their base to eliminate an appealing shelter area for small animals that are likely to gnaw on young wood. Due to weathering, decomposition, and other environmental factors, additional amounts of organic mulch may be needed from time to time.

Fertilizer

When nutrients are supplied to a plant through the soil (they can be furnished through the bark or as a foliar spray), they become fertilizers. Initially, fertilizers were organic—manure, plant residue, ground bones, and blood meal. However, synthetic organic and inorganic fertilizers became popular when industry provided more options by synthesizing, manufacturing, mining, and packaging them for convenience. Today, as a consciousness develops toward the use of natural resources, we are returning to organic recyclable materials.

Fertilizers replenish soluble salts (combination of elements). If at any time the soil becomes deficient in any one of the numerous minerals (such as nitrates as a source of nitrogen, phosphate as a source of phosphorus, and compounds containing potassium, calcium, iron, magnesium, and aluminum), fertilizers can replace them. However, using any single element or a combination of elements contributes to a higher level of soluble salts that, in excess, can damage plants and organisms in the soil. Fertilizers should be used cautiously and sparingly.

CHARACTERISTICS AND USE OF FERTILIZERS

1. Fertilizers may be natural, synthetic organic, or inorganic depending on their source and composition. Natural organic and synthetic organic fertilizers are composed of compounds with a carbon-based structure. Natural organic fertilizers are derived from animal or plant by-products. Synthetic organic fertilizers are similar in structure but are man-made. Inorganic fertilizers neither have a carbon structure nor are they derived from living matter. Regardless of where fertilizers come from, they have to be in a water soluble form to be taken up by plant roots. Inorganic fertilizers usually dissolve readily in water (except those that are designed to be slow release). As a result, they are quickly available for root absorption. Organic fertilizers are often weakly or not at all soluble in water. They become usable either by chemical reaction with water (hydrolysis) or through decomposition of soil microorganisms. Soil characteristics, pH, temperature, and moisture all influence how quickly they become available. Regardless, organic fertilizers break down from complex compounds to the same nutrient salts that are provided by inorganic fertilizers; that is, plants absorb nitrogen as nitrates or ammonium salts whether the initial fertilizer source was organic or inorganic (Figure 4.14). In an ecological sense, the difference between organic and synthetic or inorganic fertilizers lies in how much it costs in natural resources, mining, and habitat disruption to manufacture them.

2. Fertilizers or their by-products dissolve in soil water. If too much fertilizer is applied, high salt concentrations outside the plant cell cause the cell membrane to reverse the flow of water and the cell experiences a physiological drought. "Fertilizer burn" or scorched foliage is the visible symptom of dehydration within the plant (Figure 4.15).

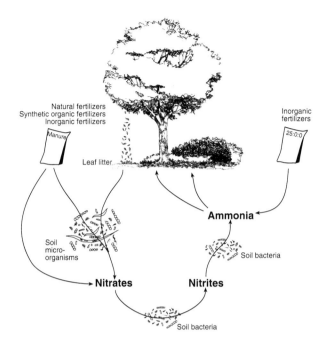

Figure 4.14—Nitrogen from different sources.

Figure 4.15—Burn—a visible symptom of overfertilization.

3. Adding nutrient elements to the soil is no guarantee that they will be accessible for plant use. Soil acidity and alkalinity affect the formation of soluble and insoluble compounds. Nutrient elements are available to a plant within a certain pH range. If the pH is too high or too low, a specific nutrient, particularly a micronutrient (those that are used in very small amounts), may not be consumable by the plant. For example, with a high pH, iron and manganese become unavailable (*Figure 4.16*). With a low pH, manganese and aluminum are available, but too much can be toxic. Plant species vary in their response to pH. Rhododendrons and plants in the heath family prefer acid soil; plants in the pea family such as honey locust, beans, and peas prefer neutral to alkaline pH (see Chapter III).

4. All fertilizer elements are susceptible to leaching, that is, moving to lower, unreachable layers in the soil. Leached materials are waste and find their way into groundwater, where they may adversely affect plants, animals, or even people.

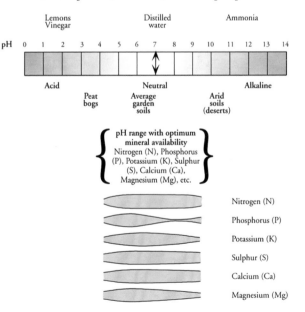

Figure 4.16—Nutrient availability and soil pH.

5. Volatilization can occur when nitrogen sources convert to ammonia gas and ultimately are lost to the atmosphere. This is more likely to occur in dry, nonfertile soil under warm temperatures. More than 25 percent of the applied nitrogen can be lost and become a pollutant in the atmosphere.

PROPERTIES OF ORGANIC AND INORGANIC FERTILIZERS

- Organic fertilizers include activated sewage sludge, manure, dried blood, cottonseed and bone meal, poultry litter, and fish scraps. Because they are generally not soluble in water initially, they are less likely to leach past the root zone, less likely to cause foliage burn (unless very fresh), and are longer lasting (four to eight weeks). They depend on microorganisms for release and a soil temperature higher than 55°F.

- Synthetic organic fertilizers consist of chemically combined forms of nitrogen such as urea-formaldehyde. Technically, urea is organic because it contains carbon and derives from bird manure. But it is also produced synthetically. (Urea is a by-product of mammals getting rid of excess nitrogen as evidenced by "burn" spots in a lawn caused by female dogs.) Organic synthetics vary in characteristics. They are water soluble, have moderate to low leaching potential, low to high burn potential, rapid to moderate low temperature response, and short to moderate residual effects.

- Inorganic fertilizers include ammonium nitrate, calcium nitrate, ammonium sulfate, potassium nitrate, and potassium chloride. Generally, inorganic formulations are soluble in water, release elements quickly, and have a higher burn and leaching potential. They are usually less expensive. Urea and inorganic forms of nitrogen can be converted to ammonia, which may volatilize when applied under warm, dry conditions. Nitrogen from an inorganic source is not affected by temperature, yet the burn potential is high. Once beyond the root zone, nitrates continue to move through the soil and into the groundwater. Avoid leaching when using quick-release fertilizers by applying small amounts.

- Controlled-release fertilizers derive from natural, synthetic organic, or coated materials. Slow-release sources may require microbial, chemical, and/or physical breakdown. The advantages of controlled-release fertilizers are that: a) nutrients are not available all at once, reducing the risk of burn; and b) fewer applications are needed, therefore, reducing the risk of leaching, volatilization, and pollution.

ANALYSIS AND GRADE
Fertilizers are sold as either "complete" or "incomplete." A complete fertilizer contains sources of the macronutrients nitrogen, phosphorus, and potassium. An incomplete fertilizer contains only one or two of these elements.

Figure 4.17—
Fertilizer analysis.

Other nutrients, such as iron or magnesium, may be present, but they are not considered in the classification.

By law, packaged fertilizers must display a product label showing the guaranteed minimum (grade) percentage of N, P, K—nitrogen, phosphorus (phosphate), and potassium (potash). Any element missing from the formulation is represented by zero. Ammonium nitrate (NH_3SO_4), 21-0-0, does not contain phosphate or potash. A fertilizer with a grade of 16-16-16 consists of 16 percent nitrogen, 16 percent phosphorus, and 16 percent potassium (*Figure 4.17*).

Figure 4.18—Remains after mining a mountain.

FERTILIZER FORMULATIONS

Fertilizers are available in liquid, solid, or timed-release form and all perform equally. Liquids are fluids in which the nutrients are in a solution. Dry formulations are granules or powder and are usually less costly. Most nitrogen sources in dry fertilizers are also available in liquid form.

FERTILIZERS FOR PLANT GROWTH

If we knew or thought about what is involved in mining, manufacturing, packaging, and transporting fertilizers, we would configure our landscape designs and maintenance practices more responsibly (*Figure 4.18*). There are choices we can make to reduce the need for additional fertilizers and our dependence on methods that contribute to air and groundwater pollution.

WAYS TO REDUCE THE NEED FOR FERTILIZERS

- In general, most soil is fertile enough as it is for trees and shrubs, possibly because mycorrhizae (special fungi that live in and on plant roots) help plants exploit larger volumes of soil. Avoid overwatering, compaction, harmful chemicals, pollution, and excessive fertilizer use that may harm the mycorrhizae and other microorganisms. Use the least toxic, but most effective materials (*Figure 4.19*).
- Micronutrients are usually sufficient in existing soil, unless it is excessively alkaline or sandy. Iron deficiencies are rarely caused by lack of iron in the soil; they

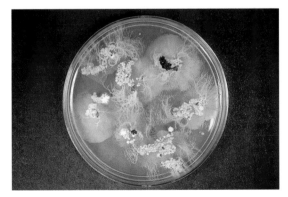

Figure 4.19—Microorganisms that live in soil.

develop because iron is chemically tied up in unavailable forms due to a high pH (alkalinity). If you select plants based on soil type, fertilizer may not be necessary. Soil pH is an important gauge of what you can grow.

- Every plant part—leaf, flower, fruit, stem, or root—harvested from the soil takes some nutrients with it. Design to allow plant residue to remain in the soil and decompose in place, or compost it for reuse (*Figure 4.20*).

Figure 4.20—Plant residue that could be used and not trashed.

- Most potassium deficiencies in lawns have been attributed to removing grass clippings or excessive leaching due to irrigation. Allow clippings to remain on the lawn; water only to the root zone.

- Although nitrogen makes up 78 percent of the atmosphere, it is not available for plants until certain soil bacteria convert it into nitrates or ammonia. Most of these bacteria live in the soil or in root nodules of specific plants. Alder, buffalo berry, and many plants in the pea family such as clover "fix nitrogen." These plants can supply themselves with a natural nitrogen source in nonfertile or sandy soil. If fertilizer is required for sandy soil, split the applications to avoid nitrogen loss from leaching (*Figure 4.21*).

- Reduce leaching by watering carefully. Apply water to moisten the root zone and not beyond (see Chapter VI on irrigation). Do not apply any more fertilizer than what is recommended.

- Phosphorus is one of the major causes of excess algae growth in lakes and a major pollutant of groundwater. Organic phosphorus from plant material is soluble and leached from plant debris found in gutters and streets, becoming part of the runoff. Sweep up plant debris and compost it.

- Use discretion when applying any fertilizer. Too much potassium inhibits the up-

Figure 4.21—Root nodules of nitrogen fixing alders.

take of nitrogen and calcium. Too much nitrogen stimulates lush leaf and stem growth, reduces root development, lowers carbohydrate reserves, and increases susceptibility to environmental stresses such as freezing and disease. Overfertilization can reduce root growth in favor of shoot growth. This subsequently increases the total leaf area and the potential of reducing overall drought resistance.

- Do not use complete fertilizers unless needed. Individual nutrient elements should be applied separately to avoid unnecessary use. Herbicides combined with fertilizer are not recommended.
- Accepting a lower growth rate can supplant or minimize fertilizer use.

When to Fertilize

Except when advised by a professional, fertilizer should not be needed on more mature trees and shrubs. On other plants, nitrogen is often the only nutrient necessary. Fertilizer should be applied only if the plant needs it and when it is most likely to use it. How much of one nutrient a plant needs over another depends on its stage of growth, plant size, competition, soil, and climate. Young plants require more phosphorus than mature ones. Faster growing plants require more nitrogen than slower ones.

Base the need for fertilizer on plant performance, visual clues such as lack of vigor, sparse foliage, light green or yellow leaves, twig dieback, gradual slowing of growth over a two- to three-year period, and comparison with adjacent plants. Even then the problem is likely more often due to other factors such as wet or dry soil, insect damage, and air pollution that cause symptoms similar to nutrient deficiency. Consider other external environmental effects first.

Fertilizers should be applied right before new growth begins (late winter or early spring). Cool-season grasses, often weakened from summer stress, respond well to fertilization in late summer/early fall when their roots are active. Fertilizing too early or too late may encourage succulent growth that is damaged by freezes. Again, returning clippings to the lawn can greatly reduce or even eliminate the need for fertilizers.

When in doubt, seek professional advice and/or get a soil test.

CHAPTER V

Planting and Development, Health, and Maintenance

Planting

The goal in planting is establishment—that is, getting the roots to grow into the surrounding soil as soon as possible. For this to happen, two conditions need to exist: a healthy root system and a welcoming soil environment. Heathy roots are critical to plant growth because they bring in water and dissolved nutrients to the entire plant as well as serve as the site for hormone synthesis (root tips) that signals plants to grow. Whatever affects the roots affects the entire plant, namely the shoots that consist of stems, leaves, buds, flowers, and fruit. A major assault on healthy roots is transplanting because it can damage so many of them. Generally, the larger the plant, the more roots are destroyed. This can be very stressful because not only must the roots regenerate and grow, but they also still have to maintain the plant body even with a much reduced root system. Anything you do to minimize the stress of transplanting/planting increases the probability of successful establishment. Proper timing, temperature, moisture, soil environment, and careful handling all influence the successful move.

TIMING AND TEMPERATURE

The most favorable time to plant is (a) when transpiration is low (generally when the plant is dormant or inactive); (b) when root regeneration is high—usually in spring, sometimes in late summer to early fall when soil temperatures are between 55 and 75°F; and (c) when there is sufficient moisture for new cells and tissues to develop, usually in spring, sometimes fall (although irrigation can provide the necessary moisture).

Although the optimum temperatures for root growth lie between 55 and 75°F, roots will grow between 40 and 90°F. With the exception of bare root plants that have a narrow window of planting time in early spring before bud break, balled and burlapped and container plants can be planted at other times of the year. However, when plants have fresh succulent growth as in the summer, planting is more risky and requires more water and careful monitoring. Plants can also be planted when the temperatures are not much above freezing, as long as moisture is available and the roots do not freeze. To save water and minimize risk, plant when natural conditions are most favorable. Rule of thumb: If you are planting in the first half of the year, allow at least six weeks before bud break and before the expected periods of summer heat stress; if you are planting in the second half of the year, allow for six weeks after the summer's heat begins to subside when top growth is nearly complete and four to six weeks before soil temperatures reach 40°F.

Generally root regeneration is optimal in spring, but there are exceptions and differences among plant species. Plants that are the easiest to transplant usually undergo relatively shorter periods of root regeneration and can be planted in spring or fall or at other times when conditions permit. Ashes and elms are two examples. Other plants such as magnolias regenerate roots in spring and should only be planted then. Some perennial species such as bearded iris and oriental poppy are planted in summer during their resting stage; bulb crops such as tulips, daffodils, and crocus are planted when fully dormant in fall to early winter.

PLANT ESTABLISHMENT

Plants are not fully established until vigorous twig or top growth returns. For herbaceous plants, this may take one to several weeks; for trees and shrubs, this can take a month to several years. Larger woody plants with more root damage will take longer. The estimated time for trees dug in the field is five to twelve months per inch of trunk diameter. That is, a 2-inch diameter tree will take two years to establish and a 5-inch diameter tree will take five years. Trees dug from the field for transplant (balled and burlapped) take longer to establish because 90 to 95 percent of their roots are left behind (*Figure 5.1*). Estimated establishment time for container grown plants is one to two months per inch of trunk diameter because their roots, for the most part, are kept intact. To establish trees more quickly (all other conditions being equal), generally select smaller specimens (less than 2$\frac{1}{2}$ inches in diameter).

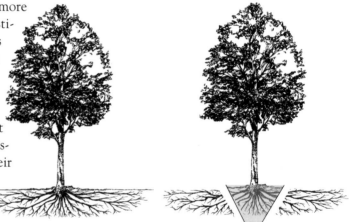

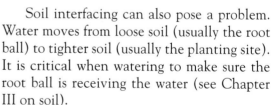

Figure 5.1—Trees dug from the field lose 90 to 95 percent of their roots.

SOIL AND PLANTING

Plant roots establish freely in porous soil where there is available moisture. If they are forced to establish in tight soil, heavy clay, compacted sites, or dry environments, they may exhaust their stored energy before they can photosynthesize.

Soil interfacing can also pose a problem. Water moves from loose soil (usually the root ball) to tighter soil (usually the planting site). It is critical when watering to make sure the root ball is receiving the water (see Chapter III on soil).

HANDLING PLANTS

When handling the plant, try not to damage the roots or shoots. Always pick it up by its container or root ball and not by the trunk or young stems. If the plant comes with planting guidelines, take the time to read them carefully.

CHECKING SOIL DRAINAGE

Before planting the site, check the soil for drainage and hardpans (see Chapter III on water drainage). If water drains slowly, you have several options:

1) Select plants that tolerate saturated soil for a period of time, such as bottomland species. Do not plant evergreens as they are more sensitive to poor drainage than most deciduous plants.

2) Try to drain the area with drain tiles (*Figure 5.2*).

3) Dig a trench that helps transport excess water from the soil ball to several feet beyond grade. The trench can be filled with pea gravel (*Figure 5.3*).

4) Depending on plant size, raise the planting area by placing the plant on top of the ground and surrounding it with soil (*Figure 5.4*). Note that raised beds mean less soil volume and less insulation. Roots may be more vulnerable to freezing temperatures. For raised beds and container plantings, select plants for a lower hardiness zone than is recommended for your area (*Figure 5.5*).

5) If there is an elevated water table due to hardpan, try to break through the impervious

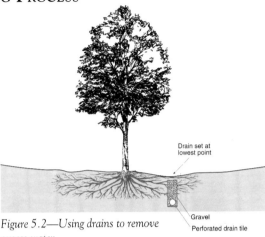

Figure 5.2—*Using drains to remove excess water.*

Drain set at lowest point
Gravel
Perforated drain tile

Trench to remove excess water

Figure 5.3—*Trenching may transport excess water from soil.*

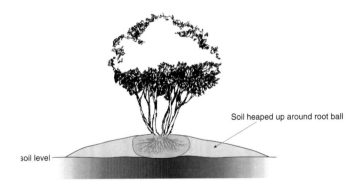

Soil heaped up around root ball
Soil level

Figure 5.4—*Raising the soil above grade around the plant ball.*

Figure 5.5—*Raised planter with Siberian pea shrub— hardiness Zone 2 in hardiness Zone 5.*

layer with a pick, shovel, or drill to enable the water to drain.

6) Be practical. You may simply have to use this area for something else.

DIGGING THE HOLE

Before digging the hole, make sure that all underground utilities have been accounted for. You can call your utility company to mark the lines. Avoid digging the hole too deeply. Measure the root ball first. The bottom of the hole should be on solid ground because loose soil at the bottom of the hole allows the plant to settle below grade where excess water from adjacent areas may collect. If you are lucky enough to have sandy loam, a hole deep and wide enough to fit the root ball is sufficient. However, in urban/suburban environments, this is unlikely unless the soil has been thoroughly amended or has matured over many years. Under most urban/suburban conditions, the planting hole should be 1 to 2 inches shallower than the root ball and at least two to three (or more) times wider than the root ball. Wide holes allow roots an aerated area to become established outside the original root ball. In most cases, the roots eventually grow into adjacent sites. The planting hole should also have sides that slope toward the bottom (*Figure 5.6*). Bare root plants need a hole wide and deep enough to provide ample space for the roots to spread without crowding.

Trees and shrubs perform at their worst where the soil depth is 5 inches. They grow better in 10 inches of soil, much better in 16 inches, and best in 20 to 30 inches. In the landscape, increasing soil volume for root growth in order to encourage extensive lateral spread will provide

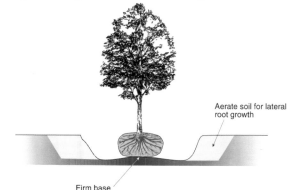

an environment for healthier plants (*Figure 5.7*). Avoid container-type holes with no room to grow and planters that restrict growth.

Aerate soil for lateral root growth

Firm base

Figure 5.7—Increasing soil volume to encourage lateral root spread.

CHECKING SOIL INTERFACE

Before planting, take note of the two soils you're working with (the root ball soil and the soil on the site). Which soil has the finer texture—the one surrounding the roots or the one on the site (see Chapter III). Generally plants grown in field soil (usually a clay loam) are more likely to come with soil similar to your planting site and the interface between the two soil types may not be that great. However, container soil usually has more organic and inert materials and is most likely very different

Figure 5.8—Death of plant due to different soil textures; plant's roots did not move out of root ball.

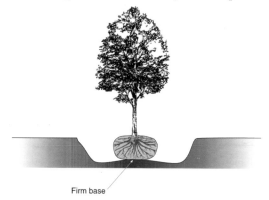

Firm base

Figure 5.6—Planting hole with firm base and sloped sides.

from the planting site. Placing soils together with very different textures will result in water attraction to one and loss to another. The tighter soil (generally, the site) will attract water at the expense of the coarser soil (the container). Several months later, the plant will show decline because the root ball dried out. To avoid this, aerate the soil on the site and roughen the roots of the plant so they can branch into the surrounding soil. Then water directly into the root ball (*Figure 5.8*).

PLACING THE PLANT

Avoid overhandling the plant. Once in the hole, it is harder to shift around, especially plants that are balled and wrapped. Before placing the plant in the hole, decide how you want it to look and then, ideally (particularly with heavy trees), it will slide in with minimal damage to the root ball. Do not place the plant lower than the grade level at which it was growing. You can discern the grade level by checking a dark stain on the trunk noting the demarcation between root and trunk. Do not rely on the point at which the burlap or materials is tied because it can be much higher than the original soil line. Plants are heavy and the soil ball can break. Whatever holds the ball together (wire, burlap, or plastic) should be removed after the plant is fully situated in the hole. Remove the material from the top and sides, but not beneath. If the soil ball begins to crumble, you may need to cut the

Figure 5.9—Remove whatever holds soil ball together once tree is in hole.

material off in pieces. If the soil is glazed (either in the root ball or side walls of the planting hole), make shallow slices in it. Avoid damaging the root ball (*Figure. 5.9*).

With container plants, loosen the plant by pushing down on the outside with the container on its side. Gently shake the plant loose. If the

Figure 5.10—Loosen or core encircling roots.

plant soil is bounded by matted roots, carefully loosen them and prune encircling ones so they will not continue following the same path once in the planting hole (*Figure 5.10*).

Once the plant is properly situated, fill the hole with soil by gently firming it around the plant, eliminating any large air pockets. Do not stomp or compact the soil. The soil that goes into the hole is the same soil that was removed. Most research shows that soil amendments added to backfill soil in the hole do not improve plant establishment, and, in some cases, may be detrimental. This is, in part, because roots may stay in the amended soil. For the establishment and growth of greater root systems, roots need to move into adjacent areas. If the soil is extremely poor you may need to amend a large area (see Chapter III on amendments). When planting a single plant, the most beneficial thing you can do is provide an aerated area for the roots to grow and a soil that drains well. Remember to dig a wide hole where plant roots have room to expand. Eliminate any hardpans or barriers to water movement. Once planted, form a collar 2 to 3 inches high around the hole to help retain water during establishment *(Figure 5.11)*. Remove this ridge once the plant is established.

Should the hole need to be dug in advance of planting (which is helpful to reduce the time the plants are exposed), dig the hole and mulch it with wood chips or straw until planting time. If it is in cold weather, cover the soil to prevent freezing. Remove the mulch at planting time.

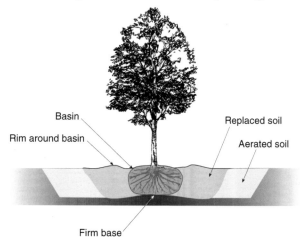

Figure 5.11—Form a rim 2 to 3 inches high around the planting hole.

WATERING THE PLANT

Immediately after planting, the plant should be watered well. Wash the soil down so that it makes contact with the roots. Again, watch for the interface, making sure water gets to the root ball. After the plant is in the ground, it is also possible and very common to overwater the root ball. Check soil moisture before watering. The first year or two for trees and shrubs is critical. Watering should be monitored carefully until the roots have grown into the surrounding soil at least 1 inch. Fertilizing during establishment is generally not necessary. You may be able to observe plant establishment by watching the vigor of the plant, or you may have to dig into the surrounding soil to see if the roots have grown into it. Water stress on newly planted materials (especially small plants) can be in-

tense in only one or two days if the temperatures are high and the relative humidity low. Young herbaceous transplants such as bedding plants or young seedlings can desiccate in a few hours if there are strong winds, low relative humidity, and high temperatures. If necessary, shade or protect them from winds during this time.

SECURING AND STAKING TREES

Securing a small tree in place with stakes or guy wires is usually unnecessary, unless in a windy or wet area where it really needs some temporary support. In some instances, staking has proven to be detrimental. It can cause bark damage, inhibit wind resistance, and reduce the normal trunk taper. Avoid it where possible. If a tree is too tall to stand alone until it is established, it should be staked. Use soft materials in order not to damage the cells underneath the young bark. Two to three stakes in the ground spaced equal distances apart outside the perimeter of the planting hole are sufficient. The stakes need to be removed as soon as the tree has rooted in *(Figure 5.12)*.

WRAPPING TREE TRUNKS

Using special tree wrap to protect young smooth bark from winter daytime sun and cold nights has been a standard horticultural practice. However, research is now showing that temperature fluctuations may be greater under wrapped trees. There are other ways to

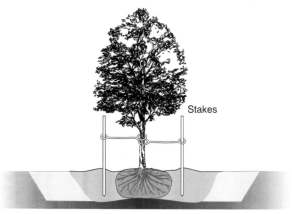

*Figure 5.12—Secure a tree **only** if necessary.*

safeguard young, smooth bark from direct sunlight in winter. Shade the trunk by grouping shrubs to block the sun, plant multistemmed specimens so the sun does not strike the trunk at a direct angle, or set up a temporary structure of burlap to shade the trunk. If you feel more comfortable with wrapping or until more research is available, wrap the trunk after leaf fall and remove it as soon as the new leaves emerge (*Figure 5.13*).

Figure 5.13—Shade the tree trunk by screening with shrub plantings.

Plant Development, Health, and Maintenance

The primary goal in landscape maintenance is to preserve the integrity of the design and maintain plant health. Preserving the integrity of a design is a lot easier when the plants perform the way they are supposed to. Successful plant performance is a result of appropriate selections for the design and site. Plant health is easier to sustain when you have a basic understanding of how plants grow, what they need, and what causes stress. Stress in any plant is a disruption of their normal growth activities.

PLANT GROWTH

Plants grow throughout their lifetime in height, length, and width. No matter what type of plant (woody or herbaceous), the roots and shoots have specific areas that remain young forever because they possess the potential for new growth. Other than their resting stage (dormancy), these areas continually divide and produce new cells. In herbaceous plants, they are located at the tips of roots and shoots (buds and stems), allowing the plant to grow in height and length. In woody plants, they are located at the tips of roots and shoots and also on the outer part of stems and roots, enabling woody areas to grow in girth. Any time there is damage to a particular growing point, the consequence usually is no more growth in that area (*Figure 5.14*).

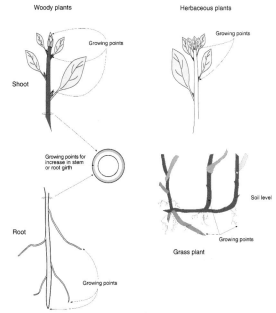

Figure 5.14—Growing points of woody and herbaceous plants.

ROOTS

Roots are major plant organs that we often ignore because they are normally out of sight and underground. However, their role is critical to the health of the plant. Not only do they anchor the plant and keep it from toppling over, but they also absorb and transport minerals and water to the rest of the plant as well as store food.

There are several categories of roots: taprooted or fibrous systems and herbaceous or woody. Taproot systems comprise a few main, large roots with some smaller branching ones. As a rule, these plants are more challenging to transplant than plants with fibrous root systems. Fibrous root systems lack major, large roots, but form a continuous branching of roots (*Figure 5.15*). Behind the root tips are smaller roots and root hairs. These are very slender, thin, and threadlike and play a critical role in absorbing water and dissolved minerals. These roots are mostly herbaceous (nonwoody), short-lived, regenerate continually, and are vulnerable to wet, dry, or excessively hot soil. In addition to root hairs, behind the root tips on nearly all plants are fungi strands called "mycorrhizae." These represent a special symbiotic relationship between certain soil fungi and roots (*Figure 5.16*). Mycorrhizae

Figure 5.15—Fibrous and tap-rooted systems.

Figure 5.16—Mycorrhizae represent a special relationship with plant roots.

Figure 5.17—Anchor and transport roots.

absorb nutrients from the soil and transport them to the plant; carbohydrates from the plant are then transferred to the fungus. Larger roots in trees and shrubs tend to become woody, some forming the basic anchoring and transport structure that is more likely to survive throughout the lifetime of the tree or shrub (*Figure 5.17*).

ROOT GROWTH

All roots (whether herbaceous or woody) grow in length from their tips. Nonherbaceous (i.e., woody) roots in trees and shrubs grow in diameter as well. For many woody plants, root growth is most active in early spring and fall when temperatures are not excessive. Their peak growth period tends to be right before and right after active shoot growth. Planting, transplanting, fertilizing, watering, or other activities affecting plant growth and health should correspond with the intervals of root growth and dormancy. Transplanting is most successfully accomplished right before active root growth. This way the roots can reestablish in their new site. In addition, water and nutrients (fertilizers) should be applied when roots are actively growing and not when they are nearing their resting stage. The extent to which root systems grow depends on several factors: the plant's genetic makeup, temperature and season (as mentioned on page 102), soil characteristics, and soil moisture. Active root extension occurs at the very small root tips. Porous soil with adequate moisture unimpeded by barriers or compaction will enable these tips to grow freely and branch, eventually extending two to three times beyond the spread of the plant's aerial parts. When conditions are ideal and soil moisture, oxygen, nutrients, and space are all readily available, roots not only grow in length, but woody roots also grow in width, increasing their reserves. When any one of the above conditions is minimized, roots stop growing in diameter and food storage (necessary for getting plants through stressful times) is compromised.

WHAT ARE PLANT ROOTS UP AGAINST IN CULTIVATION?

- Restricted root zones from buildings and pavement, hardpans, compaction, and poor drainage (see Chapter III on soil). Trees with root systems that normally would spread about 100 feet are often confined to very restricted spaces between

Figure 5.18—Avoid restricting root growth.

curbs and sidewalks (*Figure 5.18*). To avoid this, increase the soil volume to encourage extensive lateral spread.
- Automobile and foot traffic; situate plants where the roots are protected from compaction.
- Pollutants from building materials, salt spray, and litter; choose planting sites where these materials do not accumulate or collect (*Figure 5.19*).

Figure 5.19—Plants subjected to salt spray.

- Poor soil in which transplanted root systems may never regenerate even 10 percent of the original roots. Locate plants where they are most likely to succeed.
- Removal of organic material and topsoil, resulting in poorer quality subsoil as the growing medium; take growth into consideration before planting.
- Limited moisture; select plants best suited to existing site conditions.
- Higher temperatures surrounding hard surfaces of streets and walkways; select plants best suited to the site's conditions.

SHOOTS

Shoots consisting of stems, leaves, and buds are the major aboveground plant parts. Each shoot contributes to the production and transport of sugars (photosynthates) to the roots and to the rest of the plant. They also support and frame the plant structure. Herbaceous, nonwoody plants have flexible, green stems that grow in

length, but not in width. Woody plants sustain active lateral cell division (similar to woody roots) that increases stem and trunk diameter. Buds located on the stems are small projections of undeveloped shoots, leaves, and/or flowers. In addition, unlike roots, shoots also effect cell division between the nodes where buds are attached and enable the area between the nodes (internodes) to elongate (*Figure 5.20*). Stems also store food.

SHOOT GROWTH

Plant species vary in their shoot growth. Some only have one growth spurt per year. Tissues are formed in the bud one year and expand the next year. This expansion usually occurs relatively quickly in early summer and then the tissues are done for the season. Examples of this type of growth include oak, beech, and white pine. However, if early bud expansion is interrupted (e.g., by frost), the plant can regenerate new growth later in the spring using secondary buds that were held in "reserve." Sometimes as a response to stress such as defoliation, these species will produce late summer shoots. Dry summer soil will not affect the current year's growth, but may determine the number of shoots that form for the following year.

Other species such as birch, poplars, lindens, and crabapples experience two growth periods. The first growth spurt originates from buds that developed in winter. The second occurs from buds that form when the first shoots expand. Dry soil in summer will decrease shoot expansion during this second period of growth. If these types of plants need to be fertilized, it should be done during the second growth spurt, because during the first flush of growth the tissues are succulent and, hence, more vulnerable to concurrently active pathogens (e.g., fire blight bacteria).

A third type of growth is exhibited by some shrubs, southern pines, citrus, and tropical plants. These plants produce shoots in repetitive waves. The bud on a shoot opens and elongates rapidly, after which a new bud forms at the tip of that shoot. Soon thereafter, this bud opens and expands. A third or even a fourth bud may form at the end of the same shoot and expand during the same growing season. These plants sustain long seasons and continue to grow without preparing for cold temperatures. This makes them vulnerable to early snows or freezes. Any time water is withheld, shoot expansion will be diminished. Many woody plants experiencing repetitive growth waves are not cold hardy for temperate zones. Grasses also grow from shoots that continually produce, but because their growing tips are near or below-ground level, they can be mowed continually without their growing points being affected.

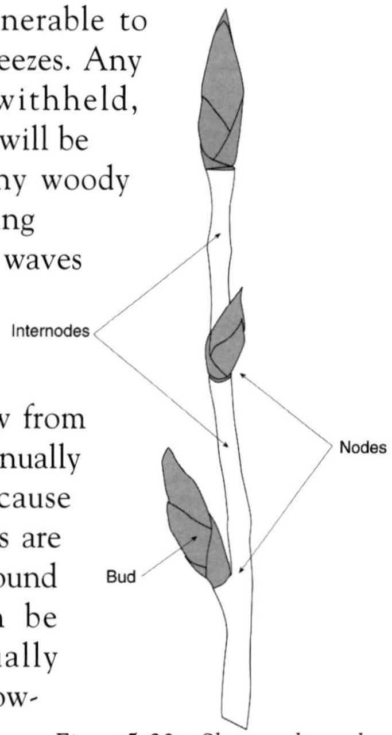

Figure 5.20—Shoot nodes and internodes.

WHAT ARE PLANT SHOOTS UP AGAINST IN CULTIVATION?

- Damage from mowers, weed eaters, heavy equipment, bicycles, and vandalism.
- Long photoperiods from streetlights that inhibit preparation for dormancy (see Chapter I).
- Air pollution and acid rain that damage cells and inhibit many physiological processes.
- Heat and light radiation from hard surfaces of asphalt and concrete raising ambient air temperatures 10 to 30°F. High temperatures are potentially injurious to thin, smooth bark and tender young foliage. High temperatures can result in desiccation. Small, thick leaves or leaves covered with hairs or wax are usually more tolerant of higher temperatures. Many plants from semiarid and arid regions that are already adapted to heat and dry soil should be used where heat and light radiation are concerns.

ROOTS AND SHOOTS

Between the roots and shoots, there is a continuous flow of moisture from the soil to the roots to the stems, buds, leaves, and eventually the atmosphere. The major intake of moisture is from the roots; the major outflow is through the leaves (transpiration). Transpiration is similar to evaporation in which plants release water vapor into the atmosphere from pores (stomates) in their leaves (through which they also extract carbon dioxide for photosynthesis). When there is an interruption in this flow, the system becomes less effective and the plant undergoes stress (refer back to *Figure 1.9*, page 10).

A CULTURAL GUIDE FOR GROWTH

FERTILIZING AND PRUNING

In the spring, when growth is succulent, there is no advantage to forcing growth with fertilizers. If fertilizers are necessary, they should be applied before bud break. In the fall, plants begin to develop frost resistance, which is the first stage of dormancy. Fertilization and pruning at this time can suspend dormancy and are not recommended before leaf fall. New growth will not have enough time to harden before winter. Pruning should be done in late winter before bud break or after plants are dormant.

TRANSPLANTING

Fine root growth peaks in spring. This is a good time to transplant. A few species such as magnolia do not regenerate roots in the fall. A few others (such as plane tree) often go dormant, drop their leaves, and then leaf out later, once they are watered. These species should only be planted in spring. As soon as the buds open in spring, cold hardiness is surrendered. Flower buds are not as hardy as leaf buds. Plants that break dormancy early should be planted away from reflected heat. Place them in areas that are slower to warm up. In spring, the tops of plants are usually the first part to break dormancy.

WATERING

Water trees and shrubs (if precipitation is inadequate) when they are leafing out, growing in height, beginning to flower, and developing fruit. The timing varies depending on the plant. They should also be watered when they grow in diameter, usually early to mid-August. After that, reduce watering—it is better to have plants vigorous in the early part of the growing season when they can build reserves. In areas with dry winters, water plants thoroughly in late fall, if necessary. In some environments, they may need watering at least once a month during winter.

Many herbaceous perennials are developing fruits and seeds during late summer. Once they set seeds, supplemental water can be reduced or withdrawn. Most herbaceous annuals are at the end of their life cycle and are setting seeds for another generation.

STRESS IN PLANTS

Stress in plants is a disruption of their physical processes and conditions. Generally, the disruptions stem from external factors in the environment, site, or landscape. Plant stress affects plant health, performance, and, ultimately, the quality of the landscape or garden. Stress also weakens the plant's defenses making it more vulnerable to insects and disease. Familiarity with and periodic examination of your plants are definitely worth your time, as they will alert you to any changes in the plant's health before it is too late.

TYPES OF STRESS

There are two types of stress—acute and chronic. Acute stress usually happens quickly and is short-lived, but can produce severe consequences. Improper use of chemicals, radical weather changes, insect infestation, and construction are some examples. With acute stress the damage is done, but if the plant is in good health, it can usually recover.

Chronic stress, on the other hand, lasts a long time and unless the cause is remedied, the plant begins to decline until it is removed or dies. With chronic stress, symptoms or causal factors may not be easy to detect. As often as not, the cause may be present one year and the symptoms may show up a year or more later. Poor nutrition, inadequate light, damaged or restricted roots, and dry soil can all induce a slow decline.

MAJOR SIGNS OF PLANT STRESS

- Changes in plant growth patterns over the past several years
- Continuous dieback of twigs and stems
- Yellowing of foliage, especially on one side
- Unusual or early leaf and twig color
- Abnormal areas of damaged or loose bark, often caused by mowers, weed eaters, or other mechanical means
- Unhealthy roots—brown, dry-looking roots may be indicative of dry soil or toxic chemicals; black roots may indicate wet soil or root rot

Plant problems are difficult to diagnose because similar symptoms can have distinctly different causes such as poor nutrition, disease, or pollution. Oftentimes, these various causes may hinder the plant's ability to photosynthesize resulting in decreased vigor and limiting new and replacement growth.

WATER STRESS

The cause of water stress in plants is twofold—both under- and overwatering. Any time plant demands for water exceed the supply, plants experience a water deficit. On the other hand, overwatering also causes water stress. In fact, overwatering is a greater cause of plant death than underwatering. This is especially true where soils are tight and slow to drain. Small, fibrous roots along with their associated fungi (mycorrhizae) are most responsible for absorbing water and the dissolved nutrients. However, they are short-lived and easily killed in excessively wet or dry soil. A plant's response to overly wet or very dry soil often produces the same end result. When roots are exposed to too much water and little oxygen or too little water and too much oxygen, plant leaves lose their turgor (fullness due to fluid content) and can no longer function (*Figure 5.21*). If plants exhibit a lack of turgor when the soil is wet, do not water. Aerate the soil by poking holes around the plant roots. Do not confuse a transient limpness of leaves with severe water stress. Temporary wilt due to a short-lived water deficit is quite common when afternoon temperatures are high. On

Plant rigid because of high turgor pressure within the cells.

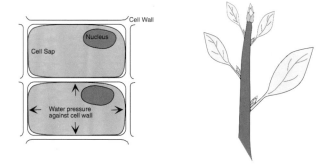

Plant wilted because of less water and low turgor pressure within the cells.

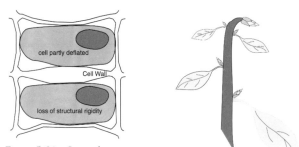

Figure 5.21—Loss of turgor.

hot afternoons, the plant is transpiring faster than water is being absorbed. Foliage may droop, but soon recovers once temperatures cool down. This is a temporary condition.

Prolonged water stress in plants reduces vigor, initiating a domino effect. When water is unavailable, leaves lose their turgor. If they lose their turgor, the stomates (pores) close. However, when stomates close, no gas exchange takes place between the plant and the atmosphere. Photosynthesis is reduced and plants are impaired in their manufacture of basic sugars. Without basic sugars, plants cannot grow new tissue. If the stress is endured, the plant eventually dies. In addition, transpiration is a plant's means of keeping its body cool. If stomates close, transpiration stops and the tissues burn. Other side effects of water stress include a buildup of toxic substances, a breakdown of protein, defoliation, nutrient deficiency, and death. A lack of sugar translates to a lack of vigor, leaving the plant more susceptible to insects, disease, and without the ability to withstand stress (*Figure 5.22*).

General signs of water stress include leaf scorch, dieback, bark blisters, a gummy effluent, and bark cracks. In deciduous trees and shrubs, signs of water stress initially affect the tops of

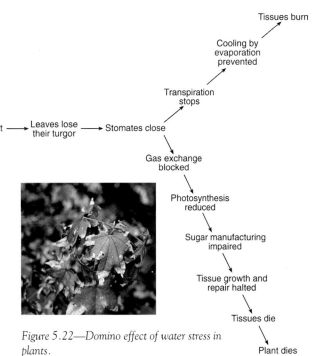

Figure 5.22—Domino effect of water stress in plants.

the plants and the tips of young shoots. In herbaceous plants, it presents as an overall wilting. With needle evergreens, the leaves, rather than wilting, may turn brown either at the tips or throughout the entire leaf. However, interior leaf drop during autumn leaf fall is normal and is not an indication of undue water stress.

WAYS TO MINIMIZE WATER STRESS

DURING DRY PERIODS

- Water when necessary, but do not fertilize or prune at times when water is scarce. These practices may stimulate growth and consequently further stress. In addition, fertilizers may accumulate in the soil and in too high concentrations will injure the plants. Pruning often forces new growth or healing tissues. Both use stored energy.

- Do not apply pesticides. They may alter, increase, or disrupt normal plant processes, and plants under stress are susceptible to injury.

- Provide shade for critical plants during the heat of the day. You can create a temporary structure with burlap attached to 2 x 2-inch stakes. This also helps reduce transpiration.

- Reduce wind by setting up temporary windbreaks, which will help reduce transpiration.

- Mulch areas where the soil is bare. Although mulch will not reduce transpiration, it does retard evaporation from the soil as well as keep soil temperatures cooler and minimize weed competition (see Chapter IV).

- Remove undesirable plants that compete for water and nutrients.

- Some recommend antitranspirant sprays to reduce transpiration; however, these need to be applied *before* plants are stressed.

IF WATER RESTRICTIONS EXIST
- Hold back on water early in the season so plants do not grow more than they can handle.
- Designate high-priority plants versus low-priority plants. This is a subjective decision. High-priority plants should be watered first.
- Trees in new environments are particularly vulnerable to water stress for the first three to four years. Older trees generally develop larger root systems that extend two to three times farther than their canopy spread. This enables them to access more water.
- Apply water slowly, allowing it to soak in and thus reducing evaporation and run-off.
- Under water restrictions, you may need to remove one plant in order to save another. Sod competes with young trees, so remove any sod that is growing around them.

STRESS CAUSED BY INSECTS AND DISEASE

In a natural ecosystem, all organisms have a place in the food chain. One organism eats while another gets eaten—important roles in population control. For example, in a prairie ecosystem, plants produce seeds, a mouse eats the seeds, a snake eats the mouse, and an eagle consumes the snake. Once organisms die, other food chains are activated. Fungi, bacteria, and nematodes, among others, break down tissues to their very basic elements. This is the natural way—the flow of energy through the intricate links of food chains (*Figure 5.23*).

In a man-made environment, we occasionally see some of the links taken out of context.

For example, a beetle is inadvertently brought to North America and feeds on the American elm. Piggybacking along with the beetle is a fungus that also feeds on the elm. Neither pest has any natural predator controls in this country, so they proliferate. The consequence has become known as Dutch elm disease, which has resulted in the removal of thousands of American elms across the temperate United States.

Organisms or plants imported either intentionally or by accident can end up as pests in our gardens or landscapes. A pest is any organism that is out of control—plants (weeds), insects, fungi, bacteria, and viruses—that either

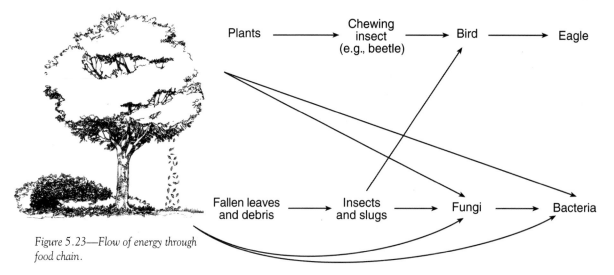

Figure 5.23—Flow of energy through food chain.

destroys the health, minimizes the vigor, or mars the aesthetics of the plants in our landscape. We then spend excessive amounts of money and energy trying to control it. Dandelions, bindweed, Canadian thistle, chestnut blight, starlings, pigeons—do these sound familiar?

INSECTS

There are three ways in which insects feed on plants. Some chew on the tissues of roots, leaves,

Figure 5.24—Chewing and sucking insect damage.

Ingredients for an Infectious Disease

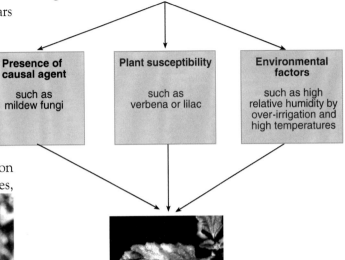

Figure 5.25—Ingredients for an infectious disease

twigs, buds, flowers, and fruit; others bore into the wood under the bark; and others suck juices from the various plant parts. In certain instances, insects are vectors and transmit fungal, bacterial, or viral diseases or they create an entry for microorganisms. In general, most insects are beneficial and some are even essential to the soil fauna or the reproduction of numerous flowering plants. Indiscriminate use of insecticides may simply produce more problems because many beneficial insects are subsequently destroyed (Figure 5.24).

DISEASES

For infectious diseases (diseases caused by living organisms) to develop in plants, three conditions must exist simultaneously. They are: the presence of the causal agent (bacteria, fungi, or virus); a plant's susceptibility to the particular causal agent; and environmental factors (such as relative humidity, precipitation, or dry soil) that influence either the plant or the causal agent (Figure 5.25). Noninfectious diseases (which constitute more than 70 percent of plant problems in urban environments) are caused by

Figure 5.26—Bacterial fire blight can often look like frost damage.

poor nutrition, temperature extremes, pollution, fluctuation in moisture, poor planting sites, and acid rain. Both infectious and noninfectious diseases produce similar symptoms. For example, twig dieback may be a symptom of bacterial fire blight or cold temperatures; black roots may be caused by wet soil or root-rotting organisms; entrées for wood-rotting organisms may be created by lawn mowers, fire, or small mammals *(Figure 5.26)*.

In the natural environment, we rarely notice these symptoms, unless the system is out of balance and a large number of plants in the ecosystem are affected. In the urban environment, we are more aware because we have a different set of standards. If the problem is not severe, we can choose to ignore it and, in some instances, wait it out, or we can aggressively attack the causal agent. We can also develop an attentive prevention program and diversify our plant selections to avoid plant-to-plant infections.

Response to Pests—Pesticides

For a while, the most popular response to pest infestations was the use of pesticides. Pesticides are legal poisons. They kill the infecting organism by contact or after ingestion. However, when applied to the foliage, other organisms can also be harmed, not to mention their contribution to air and ground pollution. When poisons are applied to the soil, they become attached to the soil particles. With clay and organic matter, they form strong attachments; sand exhibits a weaker attachment. When a pesticide is held tightly to the soil particle, it cannot be taken up by targeted plant roots and its effectiveness is minimal. In this case, the manufacturer of the chemical may recommend higher application rates, increasing the potential for harming more of the beneficial soil organisms. Sometimes a pesticide meant to target one organism is released later in large amounts causing injury elsewhere (nonpoint pollution). For example, broadleaf herbicides used on lawn weeds may be absorbed by tree roots. Other issues involving pesticides include (a) weather variations (some may prompt quicker, slower, weaker, or stronger reaction times depending on relative humidity); (b) incorrect application rates; or (c) too much water after application, spreading the agent too thinly, damaging nontarget species, and/or contaminating groundwater. In addition, although often overlooked, there are thousands of soil organisms that are affected or killed by chemical pesticides *(Figure 5.27)*. Check with your cooperative extension service with any questions you may have before applying any pesticides.

Figure 5.27—Example of beneficial soil organisms.

Alternative Responses to Pests— Integrated Pest Management

Alternative methods of dealing with pests and disease include an integrated program that encompasses a variety of techniques. The basic principle is to monitor the plants to see if there is a problem and determine if and when the infestation has reached an intolerable level. The mere presence or sign of a pest does not mean something has to be done. Improving plant health in general often enables the plant to deal with the problem on its own. Natural controls can be improved by diversifying plant materials, thus preventing a pest from spreading from plant to plant. Diversification also offers natural predators and parasites of the pests other food sources and shelter to tide them over. Not responding to pests with chemicals (in some cases) can also mean avoiding serious disruptions in natural controls. Promote plant health and vigor by appropriately siting and carefully selecting plants. Prevention is fundamental to any plant health concern.

When deciding whether to control a pest or not, ask yourself the following questions:

- What part of the plant is being affected? Is it a part that is to be harvested? (If so, you should *not* use a pesticide.)
- Can the pest be ignored?
- Is the plant healthy enough to tolerate the damage? Vigorously growing plants can tolerate some leaf loss without permanent damage.
- If the pests are plants, will they seed and become more invasive?
- Are there natural controls present that may keep the situation in check? (Many external controls are unnecessary since insect populations rise and fall between seasons. Note that everything has its place and try not to overreact.)
- If the pests are insects, are they young enough, or is it early enough in the season to have the potential to cause more injury later on? (If this is the case, a more aggressive response may be necessary. Many times a pest is detected when it is in its terminal stage about to stop feeding, and by then, it is too late to do anything that would be of use.)
- Are control options worth the effort? (Often only a small percentage of insects ever reach the adult stage.)
- Will using pesticides on any vegetation limit its use in composting or recycling?

Other Controls

- Use traps that lure pests with sex attractants (pheromones) (*Figure 5.28*).
- Select only disease-resistant plants.
- Discourage a buildup of pests by rotating crops in vegetable gardens and flower beds.
- Use mechanical controls for weeds, such as mowing, burning, or hand weeding.
- Use biological controls that enlist beneficial organisms such as insects, parasites, predators, and pathogens to control pests.
- Maintain good sanitation practices and remove diseased foliage and other plant

Figure 5.28—Traps that lure insect pests.

parts. Destroy them and do not add them to the compost pile.

CHAPTER VI

Applying Water

Irrigation

In a perfect world, natural precipitation would replace soil water on demand. In a less-than-perfect world, we irrigate. The questions then asked are: how much and when should we irrigate?

Watering xeriscape landscapes can take two different approaches: one of survival, and the other of efficiency and conservation. Managing landscapes for survival is necessary when a drought or imposed water restrictions exist. Survival strategies involve using only what is necessary in order to maintain the landscape and to keep plants in an acceptable state. At this level, it may be necessary to let some plants go dormant and water only to prevent them from dying.

At the second level, landscapes are managed for water efficiency and conservation by applying and using water carefully, even if there is no visible water shortage. In this case, irrigation is applied responsibly by following some basic ground rules.

RULE 1: DO NOT RELY ON AUTOMATIC TIMERS

If you have an irrigation system, operate it manually, especially when it is raining. If you are using automatic controls, set them seasonally and adjust to weather conditions. Make sure you can override the system when natural precipitation kicks in.

RULE 2: KNOW WHEN TO WATER

Knowing when to water is challenging, knowing when *not to* is even more so. Gardeners kill more plants by overwatering than underwatering. To learn water efficiency, start with an open mind and let go of old habits. Watering skills begin with observation and inspection.

(A) OBSERVE PLANTS FOR SIGNS OF WATER STRESS

Wilt is the most obvious sign of water stress on most broad-leaved plants, but it does not manifest on evergreens or dryland species. Be alert to abnormal dropping of interior foliage, cacti contracting into the soil, foliage discoloring, shrinking tissue, and soil cracking or shrinking at the edges (*Figure 6.1*). Dig into the soil and feel around the root zone.

Most plant roots exist near the soil surface, which is also where water loss by direct evaporation is most rapid. This means that the soil initially begins to dry out at the surface and then advances to deeper layers. In areas where there is a high evaporation rate, plants with roots confined to the upper soil will either go dormant

Figure 6.1—Water stress in plants: poor color (A) and wilt (B).

first or die first. The next group of plants with deeper roots becomes dormant or dies next. In other words, there is a sequence of cessation, slowing of activity, or death due to water availability, root depth, and the progression of drying soil. In some cases, you can use herbaceous plants with larger leaves, such as sunflowers, that will indicate water stress by wilting in among higher priority plants to monitor moisture availability *(Figure 6.2)*.

Figure 6.2—Use indicator plants that show water deficits, but recover quickly. Note background plant not showing stress.

(B) OBSERVE THE SOIL

Knowing when to water means learning about soil moisture and the way soil feels, looks, and smells under different moisture levels. As an exercise, saturate the soil and let the water drain. Then take a handful of soil, squeeze it firmly to see how it feels, smells, and looks. Each day do the same thing so you can feel and see the soil change as it dries. How well the soil holds its shape when you squeeze it is an indication of how much moisture is in the soil (see Chapter III) *(Figure 6.3)*.

Figure 6.3—Detect soil moisture by observing it under several conditions: first day, soil saturatred

second day, soil drier,

third day, soil drier.

(C) ANTICIPATE WHEN TO WATER

In some cases, you can project or plan ahead if you know your plants and follow weather predictions. If dry periods are expected or warm weather is approaching, water the soil root zone thoroughly and then allow it to dry until plants begin to show signs of water stress. Once they reach this point, water again. You will need to be observant. In the fall, prepare plants for dry winters by thoroughly watering their root zone. This is especially important for evergreens.

(D) USE EVAPOTRANSPIRATION RATES AS A GUIDE

Evapotranspiration rate (ET) refers to the amount of moisture transpired from the plant (usually the leaves) and water evaporated from the soil. ET rates are available through cooperative extension services, televised weather reports, or local newspapers. They are measured in inches per month for the average requirements of a specific crop such as Kentucky bluegrass. The ET rate is influenced by temperature, relative humidity, soil, plant species, sun, shade, wind, and day length. Because conditions vary and the rates are measured for a specific crop, ET rates do not accurately translate to trees, shrubs, and other plantings in the landscape. However, as a guide, the ET rate is useful for determining how much water to replenish. It is especially helpful with cool-season lawns.

As an indicator, you can also set up your own system to give you a rough estimate of evaporation loss. Place a flat, deep pan outside filled with 6 inches of water. Measure to see how much of the water evaporates when solar radiation is most intense. Generally, maximum ET rates occur in the hottest months. The pan method estimates the potential loss rate, not the actual one (*Figure 6.4*).

(E) SOIL MOISTURE CAN BE MEASURED WITH TOOLS SUCH AS MOISTURE SENSORS AND TENSIOMETERS

Tensiometers are tubes filled with water, accompanied by a gauge that measures soil moisture tension. As the soil dries, the gauge reading is high; when soil is moist, the gauge reading is low (*Figure 6.5*).

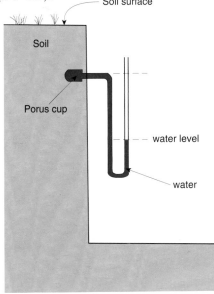

Figure 6.5—*Moisture tensiometer.*

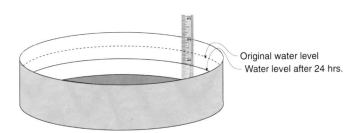

Figure 6.4—*To estimate how much water has evaporated, set a pan of water out and measure loss.*

RULE 3: WATER WHEN PLANTS NEED IT

Watering needs vary with the seasons, exposure, microclimates, plants, and soil. Change your watering patterns as the above conditions dictate. Spring and fall usually require less water, summer requires the most, and winter requires the least,

depending on natural precipitation and the environment. Application rates also should be adjusted based on temperature and natural precipitation. Although soil moisture is derived from precipitation, not all types of precipitation equally saturate soil. Slow, gentle rains are ideal, but rapid or too light a rain may not penetrate and may have little effect. This is not uncommon in desert regions. Cooler and more humid climates such as those in the northeast generally see more effective, frequent, and light rains.

RULE 4: PAY ATTENTION TO DIFFERENT MICROCLIMATES, SOIL, AND PLANTS

Southern and western exposures, all things being equal, need more water than eastern exposures. Northern exposures generally need the least. In addition, various soils and plants exert an impact as well. Sandy soil requires more water than clay, and mesic plants need more water than xeric ones.

Plants need different amounts of water, depending on what stage of growth they are experiencing. Young transplants require more frequent irrigation, but less quantity overall. More mature plants need fewer irrigations, but more water at one time. To reduce transpiration and watering of young plants, provide temporary shade and windbreaks. Mesic plants are less tolerant of water stress. They should be watered to keep the soil uniformly moist. Xeric plants should be watered thoroughly and not again until the soil is dry or plants indicate water stress.

RULE 5: FOCUS WATER ON PLANT ROOTS

Water should be directed to plant roots and not intercepted by foliage, fences, overhangs, and other obstacles. The rate of application should be slow enough for penetration without runoff. Water should drain between $1/4$ to 1 inch per hour. Depending on the soil, water may need to be applied in repeated cycles instead of over one long period. Clay soil, with its slow penetration, cannot be irrigated efficiently at one time in hot, windy weather using an overhead spray.

RULE 6: APPLY ONLY WHAT IS NEEDED

Roots do not grow in dry soil. They grow where the moisture is. Except for very shallow-rooted plants, most roots, including those of trees and shrubs, are established between 6 to 18 inches, deep. Root hairs and small, fine roots associated with mycorrhizae are mostly in the top 6 inches, where moisture and air are more abundant. Larger roots tend to thrive in the upper 2 feet and rarely extend deeper than 3 to 5 feet. They generally develop an irregular spread two or three times greater than their canopy. Trees in the landscape rarely have taproots. Rooting depth depends on existing obstacles such as bedrock, hardpans, a high water table, or a lack of oxygen. For all plants, watering should only moisten the entire root zone and no more; anything else is wasted and moves into the groundwater along with soluble salts, fertilizers, and contaminants.

The depth and extent of root development influences how long plants can go between irrigations. The deeper or more extensive the root system, the longer the interval. Soil texture, structure, and plant type all determine interval lengths between watering. Sandy soil needs watering more often than clay; mesic plants need more water than xeric plants. Whatever the plant type, dig into the soil to see how deep the roots go. Water the plants and wait twenty-four hours to check if the water has reached the appropriate depth. You can find out how long it takes to apply 1 inch of water by measuring the water accumulating in several tin cans placed within reach of the water source. Turn the water on and record the time it takes to fill the cans 1 inch. Once you know how long it takes to get 1 inch, multiply the time by the number of inches you want to apply. Then adjust the time by watering longer or less (*Figure 6.6*).

Some soil types display peculiarities that affect the efficiency of watering. For example, clay soil possesses the property of shrinking and cracking when dry and expanding when wet. Cracks in the soil are difficult to water because water runs through them without wetting the plants. With this situation, you may have to water more than once—the first time to seal the cracks and the second application to replenish soil moisture. Another way to water clay is to use a hose with water running slowly into the root zone. Water may need to be applied even more slowly on slopes. Soaker hoses are often useful for this purpose.

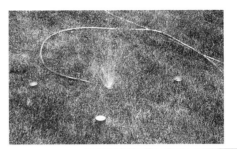

Figure 6.6— Measure accumulated water from sprinklers to gauge how long it takes to apply an inch of water.

Watering Tips for Conservation

- Water needs will vary depending upon natural precipitation. Irrigate only natural precipitation from the total amount the root zone needs before you water. You can measure natural precipitation with rain gauges placed in various spots around the landscape and then record the weekly rainfall. If you receive less than 1 inch in a week, check the soil moisture. Generally in hot weather, a cool-season lawn needs the equivalent of $1-1^{1}/_{2}$ inches of water every five to seven days; a warm-season lawn needs the same amount every three weeks; young trees need the equivalent of 1 inch every seven to ten days.
- To reduce the watering requirements of small transplants such as bedding plants, plant late in the day or early in the morning and provide temporary shade for four to seven days.
- Many plants can be sustainable using less water than when they were being watered for growth. For example, let plants go dry after harvest or be content with a-less-than-lush lawn.
- Avoid using water to clean driveways and paths—a broom works just as well.
- If moving hoses to water, use a timer to remind you when it is time to change or move a hose.
- Irrigate in early morning when wind and evaporation losses are lowest.
- Control weeds to eliminate competition for water and nutrients.

Types of Irrigation

There are many ways to irrigate. You can water by hand or use flood or basin irrigation, a sprinkler, or drip or subsurface systems. Each approach has its advantages and disadvantages. Some are easy, others are more difficult; some are cheaper, while others are more expensive; and some are more efficient, others less so. The comparisons go on and on. Most important, select what works best for you and the landscape. Irrigation materials and equipment are continuously being improved and introduced into the marketplace.

HAND WATERING

Hand watering, or what some refer to as hose dragging, is one of the more water-saving methods because overwatering demands too much of your time. Therefore, water is more likely to be applied when and where plants need it and not routinely or excessively. The disadvantage is the time it takes, as well as the lack of uniform application. Various types of sprinkling heads such as frog eyes, fan sprays, and soaker hoses are available (*Figure 6.7*). The latter supplies water at a more uniform and slower rate.

Figure 6.7—Sprinkling devices.

FLOOD/BASIN IRRIGATION

Flood/basin irrigation provides a continuous layer of water over a fairly level surface. This is an effective way of watering newly transplanted trees and shrubs. Each plant is surrounded by a circular ridge of soil 4 to 6 inches high just beyond the plant's root ball. The basin is filled with water until full; it then percolates through the soil to the root zone. Basin irrigation is also used for turf or group plantings of vegetables, annuals, and perennials where each bed is enclosed with a shallow mound high enough to enclose a specific amount of water. The method is effective in drier climates with close-growing plants on coarse-textured, well-drained soil. By design you can create rectangular beds along borders or hedges for flood irrigation. Or you can create sunken beds surrounded by mounds that serve as paths. The most important aspect of basin irrigation is to apply enough water deep enough to cover the surface and for a long enough period for the water to infiltrate and replenish what has been used in the root zone (*Figure 6.8*).

FURROW IRRIGATION

Similar to basin watering, furrow irrigation utilizes troughs placed between the plants. Water flows down the furrows and is absorbed in the soil, refilling the reservoir under the plants. This method is ideal for plants growing in rows on gentle slopes in most soils except very coarse ones. Water needs to flow slowly enough to be absorbed so as not to cause erosion (*Figure 6.9*).

SPRINKLER SYSTEMS

Mechanical methods or sprinkling systems are the most popular methods of watering because

Figure 6.8—Flood irrigation provides a continuous layer of water over a level surface.

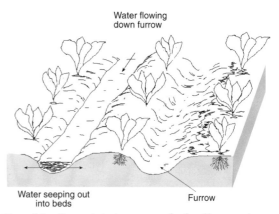

Figure 6.9—Furrow irrigation uses troughs placed between plants.

they do not require constant monitoring. They must be designed and installed according to water-saving principles to avoid common mistakes that make them inefficient and wasteful. A sprinkler system applies water in fans over a surface area. The advantage is that they (a) provide uniform plant coverage for large areas, such as lawn and low ground covers at one time; (b) control the amount of water applied, and (c) save time. However, they are only 65 to 75 percent efficient because of evaporation, wind, and interception by foliage. In addition, sprinkler systems (especially if they are poorly designed) are not selective in what they water and can end up watering such areas as driveways, streets, and sidewalks. They work best on lawns or where there is uniform vegetation. These systems should be operated in the early morning when the air is cool and calm. Lawns watered with a fine spray applied during the day can lose 40 to 50 percent to evaporation (*Figure 6.10*).

To save water with and improve your existing system, look for:

- Improper head size or shape, which can result in overspraying and runoff.
- Overpressurization, which creates fine mists of water that evaporate more readily.
- Underpressurization, which reduces uniform coverage of an area, creating dry spots.

- Inappropriate spacing of heads that are either too close, applying too much water, or too far apart, creating dry spots.
- Poor design, leading to indiscriminate watering of pavement and other things, inanimate objects, or structures.
- Slow, leaky lines or faucets that can lose significant amounts of water (100 drops per hour equates to 350 gallons per month).

DRIP IRRIGATION

Drip or trickle irrigation provides a slow and even application of water to the soil, using low-volume emitters, microbubblers, microsprays or flexible plastic tubes that are factory installed and drip water at preset intervals and at a preset rate. The system consists of main lines that carry water from the water source to precise areas and lateral lines that carry water to specific plants or crops. Each emitter (a small fitting that reduces water pressure and flow) is designed to release a specified amount of water at a given pressure. The system can be operated mechanically or automatically. Drip systems minimize evaporation, apply water only on plants and not on walks or streets, avoid too wet/too dry fluctuations, and eliminate runoff on steep slopes. The savings in water consumption over spray systems can be 50 to 70 percent. Disadvantages include (a) becoming entangled with fibrous roots of herbaceous perennials; (b) plugged lines that may go unnoticed until the plant shows signs of stress; (c) changing emitters to keep up

Figure 6.10—*Lawns watered with a fine spray applied during the day can lose half of that water to evaporation.*

Figure 6.11—*Microspray drip irrigation.*

with plant growth or new plantings; and (d) a general discomfort level and lack of understanding on the part of the operator in knowing how to use them (*Figure 6.11*).

SUBSURFACE IRRIGATION

Subsoil or subsurface irrigation works in a manner similar to drip irrigation, but is installed 4 to 6 inches underground. It supplies water to plant roots directly with little waste beyond the root zone, eliminates evaporation and the need to trim around sprinkler heads, and saves 50 to 60 percent of the water consumed compared to surface sprays. The disadvantages include (a) it may be difficult to know when problems exist (although there are ways of overcoming this); (b) it cannot be used on rocky or extremely porous soils where water will not move laterally; (c) it may be difficult to modify if the landscape changes; and (d) installation requires extreme accuracy (*Figure 6.12*).

Figure 6.12—Drip lines apply water directly to roots.

BECOMING MORE EFFICIENT WITH LAWN IRRIGATION

Maintaining a green, well-manicured lawn has become part of the American culture, but because of the growing interest in water conservation, "the lawn" has come under attack. Although irrigation can provide a near-perfect lawn, what does it actually take? The perfect green lawn needs to be growing actively and continually throughout the growing season and requires a constant supply of water, fertilizer, mowing, and edging. However, a less-perfect green lawn can still offer most of the same amenities. Settling for less will reduce water consumption, fertilizer, and energy.

WATER CONSERVATION TIPS

- Encourage an extensive root system—aerate the soil and fertilize plant roots during their peak growing period when there is natural precipitation.
- Keep the lawn green, but only water it when it begins to show some signs of stress. Become an observer. Duller than normal foliage, leaf blades that are beginning to roll, and grass that does not spring back when walked on are all signs of water stress. Check the soil by pushing a probe or screwdriver into the ground 5 to 6 inches deep. If the lawn shows resistance and/or any of the above signs, it is time to water (*Figure 6.13*).
- With warm- or cool-season grasses, reduce the need for fertilizers by proper mowing and grass recycling. Increase mowing heights. Kentucky bluegrass, blue grama, buffalo, fescues, and rye grasses all can be mowed at a height of $2^1/_2$–3 inches. Allow clippings to remain on the lawn, slowing evaporation and saving two to three applications of fertilizer per growing season.

On average, grass clippings contain 4 percent nitrogen, 2 percent potassium, and $1/2$ of a percent phosphorus as well as other nutrient elements.

- You can also reduce water use by adequately preparing a cool-season lawn for the long, hot summer. A month before hot weather sets in, discourage excessive growth by eliminating fertilizers and herbicides. Raise the cutting height of the mower half an inch. Remove only one-third of the leaf blade when mowing. Longer grass encourages deeper roots and shades the soil, thus lowering evaporation.

- To save even more water, you can let the grass slow down growth by allowing it to go dormant in summer. The contrast of green leafy trees and shrubs against light brown blades of dormant grass can be very attractive. So much "green" and what we perceive to be beautiful is due in part to what we have become used to. Note: a potential problem with summer dormancy, especially with cool-season grasses, is knowing the fine line between dormancy, and death. If a lawn changes color from green to brown, it is dormant. But if the lawn begins to thin and bare spaces develop, the grass is dying. Warm-season grasses (see Chapter II) require less water overall, and are easier to maintain in a dormant state during periods of water shortage.

- If there comes a time when serious water restrictions and rationing are imposed, set some priorities with regard to water use. You can choose to water specific areas that you use the most or those that the public sees. The rest of the lawn can then go dormant (*Figure 6.14*). You may choose to allow the lawn to go dormant and save water for trees and shrubs. Grass that normally goes dormant under heat stress revives when temperatures cool down and moisture is available.

Figure 6.13—Check moisture by pushing probe into soil 5 to 6 inches deep.

When you do water, water to moisten the root zone. In a loamy soil, it is possible to reduce the amount of applied water in alternating weeks. The first and third week, apply water 6 to 8 inches deep; the second and fourth week, apply water 3 to 4 inches deep. In clay soil where penetration is slow and on slopes where runoff is a problem, water in cycles. First water to the point of runoff, then turn the system off and let it soak in. Then water again, turn it off, and let it soak in. Continue this until the desired amount of water is applied. You can also base your irrigation on the evapotranspiration rate (ET).

- As part of the design process, plan your landscape not only to minimize lawns where they are not needed, but also to embrace flexible ways to water them. Not all areas need be watered with the same type of system nor with the same type of equipment.

Figure 6.14—Initial stages of water deficit. Note footprints and incipient dormancy on Kentucky bluegrass.

Water Harvesting

Water harvesting means collecting water and redirecting it or storing it for later use. Harvested water comes from rain, snow, or irrigation that hasn't infiltrated the soil and runs off areas such as lawns, driveways, and roofs. It can be an elaborate process, such as the Roman aqueduct system, or it can be simple like ancient people used when they created low soil ridges to channel rain and snow. We harvest water today when we create saucers around newly transplanted trees.

Overall, there is a generous amount of water that runs off your site as well as adjacent areas. The objective is to capture the runoff before it flows off the site or other areas such as at the end of a driveway. Roof eaves, lawn edges, ends of slopes, and adjacent areas are all sources of "free" water that can be better put to use in your landscape. It can either be channeled directly to plantings or it can be collected in containers and used later (*Figure 6.15*).

Figure 6.15—Collect water for later use.

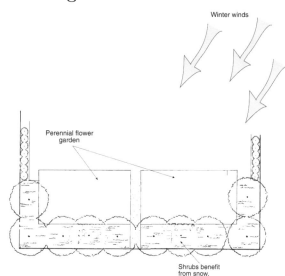

Figure 6.16—Use plants to trap snow melt.

REDIRECTING WATER FOR LANDSCAPE USE

Snow is also a source of water. On paved surfaces it melts and subsequently flows into the storm sewer system. Instead, it can be piled up in areas where moisture can be absorbed into the soil. By design, you can coordinate plantings that need winter moisture, such as evergreens, where snowmelt or water runoff is generated. Low-lying shrubs can also trap snow so that it melts into the soil (*Figure 6.16*).

Rainwater from gutters and downspouts can be redirected by placing a joint at the bottom of the downspout. A perforated pipe can then be attached to the joint to direct the water away from the house into the planted areas. Water from downspouts can also be channeled to plantings by installing a small concrete or plastic apron at the base of the downspout. Most driveways are designed to move water directly into the street (*Figure 6.17*). Depending on how the driveway or large paved areas slope, it is possible to collect and redirect this water to a planted area. If you are in the process of build-

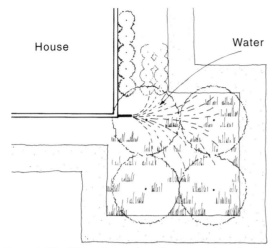

Figure 6.17—*Channel water from downspouts into planting beds or swales.*

Figure 6.18—*Intersperse hard surfaces with plantings to allow water penetration rather than runoff.*

ing a new house, the downspouts and paved areas can be designed to direct water into the landscape spread over a broad surface area.

Paved areas can be made more permeable by interspersing planting spaces between them. Not only are they attractive, but they are ideal sites for planting islands and they soften the effects of stark pavement. This approach also creates special microclimates of cooler, moist soil conducive to cushionlike plants *(Figure 6.18)*.

Slopes in the landscape are areas of potential runoff. Water can be directed to a desirable location by creating small, shallow channels. To prevent soil erosion and water runoff, keep the slopes rough-spaded and mulched until they can be stabilized with vines, fast-growing fibrous rooted plants, or suckering, colonizing plants. Steeper banks can be contoured or terraced with vertical walls of concrete, stone, or timbers *(Figure 6.19)*.

If the soil is porous, deep, and drains well, it can act as a reservoir for water. Conditions that make water storage difficult are (a) tight and/or expansive clay soil that swells when wet and shrinks when dry; (b) bedrock too close to the surface; (c) high water tables that continually keep the soil saturated with capillary water; and (d) if the soil drains slowly, the occasional downpour or the excess harvested water from natural precipitation or irrigation can be detrimental to

plant growth. For example, an excess water accumulation of 4 inches should drain within forty-eight hours. Most plants can tolerate this. However, if the water does not drain within this time, plants may be injured. In this case, you may have to decrease the amount of water that flows into the area by dispersing it to other areas. To develop a soil capable of storing excess, you may need to amend it (see Chapter III). It is possible to increase subsurface storage by introducing areas of gravel or crushed stone below the root zone. Landscapes and gardens have also been successfully designed based on storing moisture in the soil during a dormant period. Areas are planted in the spring when soil moisture is replenished through natural precipitation. This is the basis of "dryland farming"—no irrigation is necessary. You need a deep soil capable of holding soil moisture and allowing greater root penetration, natural precipitation during growing season, and large spaces between plants so they do not compete with each other.

Figure 6.19—*Terrace of level steep slopes for water retention and erosion prevention.*

COLLECTING WATER FOR LATER USE

A more familiar approach to water harvesting is to collect it in containers. A simple, easy method uses the traditional rain barrel placed under a downspout. A more elaborate system interconnects several barrels with plastic pipe near the tops as overflow for runoff from larger roofs or heavy storms. You can connect them using gravity flow, and use a submersible pump to irrigate areas nearby. Containers should be covered to retard evaporation and to prevent mosquitoes from breeding. Organic gardeners also suspend cloth bags of manure to make "green tea" as a fertilizer (*Figure 6.20*).

Figure 6.20—Suspend cloths of compost into collection container for green tea to be used as a liquid fertilizer.

More sophisticated systems of water collection that require preplanning employ cisterns made of plastic, metal, wood, or concrete, either above or below ground. The size depends on the catchment surface, which can include roofs, patios, driveways, and paths. With only 1 inch of rain, 420 gallons of water can be collected from a catchment area equaling 1,000 square feet. In a heavy storm, this may be too much water for the storage container. In this case, the excess water can resume its normal flow as if you had not harvested anything. It is important to plan for the occasional storm where there is an excess of water.

Collecting water for plant use can be applied indoors as well. While you let shower or bathwater run to warm up, collect the otherwise wasted water in buckets and use it later to water houseplants. Three quarts to 4 gallons of water can be collected at a time. It is estimated that wasted running water from two showers and two sinks can total 21 to 112 gallons per week.

For more information on water harvesting, refer to the bibliography, or call your city planner, a licensed surveyor, or a civil engineer.

Recycled Water (Gray Water)

Gray water is water you've already used in showers, baths, washing machines, dehumidifiers, and dishwashers. By recycling this water, it is possible to save an average of 100 gallons of water per day. Washing machines use 35 to 70 gallons per load; bathroom sinks supply a weekly average of 14 gallons per person. Water can be collected in buckets or via a piping system. Sink traps can be opened and hoses from washing machines can be disconnected. With a solenoid valve, it is possible to reclaim rinse water only, which is estimated at 80 to 100 gallons per week per family of four.

Because recycled water is used water, it picks up salts from soap, chlorine from bleach, as well as potentially harmful microorganisms. Sodium increases alkalinity, making the soil less permeable. Although gray water is considered safe to use on ornamental plantings, it should be avoided on vegetables, container plants, young plants, or plants sensitive to high salts and plants that require acid soil. It is recommended for use in less populated areas where it is absorbed quickly through the soil. Be aware of the detrimental effects gray water may have on soil organisms.

RECOMMENDATIONS FOR USING GRAY WATER

- Use it the same day it is collected.
- Use the rinse cycle rather than water from the wash cycle.
- Dilute it with fresh water.

- Alternate it with fresh water; do not use it continuously in one area.
- Avoid products with borax and bleach; for cleaner gray water, use simple or "organic" cleaning agents with few additives.
- Do not allow gray water to puddle on the surface.
- Protect your skin. Don't spray or sprinkle it overhead. Apply it below the surface or under a 4-inch mulch layer to minimize human contact and allow the soil to filter out harmful organisms.
- Do not let reused water flow into adjacent property, the street, or a stream.
- Do not use water that has been used to clean dirty diapers.

For more information on recycling water, contact your state department of environmental health.

Summary

By now, you have probably realized that planning a xeriscape landscape requires an intimacy with your site and a knowledge of your region. This is hard work for some and an exhilarating challenge for others. So many traditional landscapes use large amounts of turf grass maintained by programmed schedules and use power machines that contribute to air, water, and soil pollution. Excessive water use, runoff, and unnecessary fertilization also contribute. Moreover, most plant selections are made based on spatial relations and aesthetics, without taking into consideration natural associations, growing needs, and required resources.

The challenge for you lies in tailoring your design to your individual needs as well as to the environment. To do this requires a sensitivity to the region you live in and to its natural rhythms of change The result is the xeriscape you first imagined when you made the commitment to save water (*Figure 6.21*).

Figure 6.21—Xeriscape designs that reflect a sensitivity to conservation of resources, the region and its rhythms of change.

Glossary

accent—Drawing attention to a design element.

acclimate—The process of adapting to a change such as climate.

acid rain—Precipitation with a pH below 7 due to interaction of pollutants and rainwater.

adaptation—The ability to change for survival.

aeration—A way of introducing air into compacted or tight soil.

aerobic—Organisms that grow need oxygen to survive.

aggregates—The way in which individual soil particles are held together, in part determined by soil structure.

alpine tundra—Vegetation at high mountain elevations.

altitude—The height above sea level.

amendment—Material added to soil to improve drainage, moisture, or nutrient-holding capabilities.

anaerobic—Organisms that can survive in the absence of oxygen.

annuals—Herbaceous plants that go from seed to flower to fruit to seed and then die in one growing season (e.g., zinnias).

antitranspirant—A chemical spray that covers leaf pores (stomates) to reduce transpiration.

aquatic plants—Plants that grow in water; they may float on top or their roots may be growing in sediment.

arid—Climate of low relative humidity; dry conditions, such as with soil.

aridity—Lacking moisture; dry conditions.

aspect—Direction something is facing, such as a slope with north exposure.

association—Community of plants named for the dominant species (e.g., piñon/juniper woodlands).

automatic timer—Controller that automatically regulates an irrigation system.

balance—In design, an asymmetrical or symmetrical visual equilibrium among the elements of a composition.

balled and burlapped—Field-dug plant whose root ball is wrapped in burlap (or other materials).

bareroot plant—Plant without soil around roots.

base plan—Scaled plan view of land summarizing what is physically on the site, including house, property line, easements, walks, etc.

baseline—A line drawn on the plan from which to measure the distances of other structures.

basin irrigation—Water applied to a basin around the root zone of plants.

bedding plants—Herbaceous plants grown as annuals or for one season, such as tomatoes or petunias.

biennial—A plant that grows two seasons. The first season it produces leaves; the second season it produces flowers, seeds, and then dies, such as foxglove.

biological clock—Internal mechanisms that trigger physiological changes in plants.

bog—A wetland with peat as the substrate.

broadleaf evergreen—Evergreen plants with broad leaves, such as holly or rhododendrons.

broadleaf herbicide—Chemical that kills plants with broad leaves versus grass plants.

bubbler—Type of irrigation where the head bubbles water at a precise location.

bud—Projection on stem containing undeveloped shoot, leaf, and/or flower.

bulb—Modified, underground stem such as that of an onion, tulip, or daffodil.

capillary action—The interaction of water and dissolved materials with soil particles due to cohesive and adhesive properties of water.

capillary water—Water that remains around soil particles after gravitational water is gone.

cardinal temperatures—Minimum cold, maximum hot, and ideal range for plant growth and development.

catchment—A large surface area that can capture or carry water such as a driveway or roof.

chippers—Machines that break up woody materials into smaller pieces.

circulation pattern—In design, the way in which people move around a site.

clay—Very small mineral particles; less than 0.002 of a millimeter.

climate—Combination of temperature, moisture, solar radiation, and wind.

coarse-textured soil—Soil dominated by large soil particles such as sand.

compaction—Compression of soil particles together collapsing air spaces in between.

complete fertilizer—Formulations that contain nitrogen (N), phosphorus (P), and potassium (K).

compost—A mix of decayed organic matter, such as plant and kitchen waste, used as a soil amendment.

composting—The process of building compost.

conifers—Plants with seeds in cones; leaves usually needlelike such as pine or spruce.

container plant—Plants that are grown in containers rather than bare root or in the field.

contours—Lines that outline the shape or form of the land, often in reference to topographic relief.

controlled-release fertilizer—A fertilizer designed to slowly release nutrient elements for plant use.

cool-season lawn—A lawn that thrives in the cool seasons of spring and fall, but slows growth in summer.

cover crop—A short-lived crop grown to protect and improve soil characteristics.

crusting—Surface compaction that impedes water penetration.

deciduous—Woody plants that lose all their leaves at one time.

defoliation—The loss of leaves as a response to climate change or stress.

deserts—Ecosystems with low precipitation and low relative humidity.

dew—Water that condenses on cool surfaces.

dieback—Plant parts that die back, but do not kill the plant.

dormancy—A resting stage of plant growth.

dormant—Undergoing dormancy.

drip or trickle irrigation—Low pressure application of water to the soil using emitters or flexible plastic tubes that drip water.

drought—A meteorological term referring to a lack of rainfall.

dryness—A relative term describing water deficits that may be more frequent, more severe, or longer lasting than "normal"; may occur because of soil compaction, poor soil structure, and runoff.

Dutch elm disease—Infectious disease that affects many elms; transmitted by a beetle and caused by a fungus.

easement—Legal agreement giving others limited use of or access to a property.

ecological processes—Natural processes such as the cycles of nutrients and energy flow that contribute to how ecosystems function.

ecosystem—A self-sufficient, self-sustaining ecological system; the interaction between the organic and inorganic elements of the environment.

element (nutrient)—Chemical entities such as carbon, oxygen, nitrogen, potassium, or phosphorus that are necessary for plant life and growth.

elements (in design)—All objects within the landscape.

evaporation—The conversion of water from liquid to vapor; losing moisture from the earth's surface to the atmosphere.

evapotranspiration rate (ET)—The amount of moisture transpired from the plant (usually the leaves) and water evaporated from the soil. The ET rate is influenced by temperature, relative humidity, soil, plant species, sun, shade, wind, and day length.

evergreens—Plants that do not drop all their leaves at the same time.

exotic plants—Non-native species.

fertilizer—Soluble salts that are added to the soil to increase available nutrient elements for plant growth.

fertilizer burn—The visible symptom of dehydration within a plant due to high salt concentrations.

fibrous roots—Roots that continuously branch and do not develop one main structure.

field capacity—Soil that has lost gravitational water but has a full complement of capillary water; an optimal balance of water and air content ideal for plant health.

fine-textured soil—Soil that is dominated by fine soil particles such as silt or clay.

fire blight—A bacterial disease of plants such as apples, crabapples, pears, and mountain ashes.

fixed nitrogen—Nitrogen that exists in combination with other elements such as ammonium nitrate in a form that can be used by plants.

flood irrigation—See basin irrigation.

flower—A reproductive organ of flowering plants; some are very showy, others are small and difficult to see.

forest—An ecosystem that is dominated by trees.

fruit—A plant organ bearing seeds; some are fleshy such as cherry, others such as grass are dry.

furrow irrigation—Water applied in troughs between rows of plants.

geotextiles—Synthetic fabrics used as weed barriers.

germinate—Breaking dormancy, a seed sprouts new growth.

gradient—A measure of slope; the ratio between vertical distance or height and horizontal distance or length.

grasses—Plants classified in the grass family defined by specific taxonomic characteristics.

grassland—An ecosystem dominated by grasses.

gravel—Mineral particles measuring more than 2 millimeters in diameter.

gravitational water—Water that occupies the large spaces between soil particles and is subject to the forces of gravity so that it soon drains away.

gray water—Water that has been used with soaps in showers, baths, washing machines, and dishwashers.

green manure—See cover crop.

ground cover—Low-growing plants or materials used to cover large areas of soil.

groves—In a design, a grouping of trees that appear to act as a unit.

growing season—The period between the last frost of spring and the first frost of autumn; presumably, the time when plants can grow without danger of frost.

hardening off—The physiological change from a susceptible (tender) condition of summer to a resistant (hardy) one of winter.

hardiness—The ability of a plant to withstand cold temperatures without disrupting or damaging its life cycle, tissues, growth, or development; also refers to a plant's ability to withstand other environmental conditions.

hardiness zone map—A compilation of geographic regions divided into temperature degree increments representing average low winter temperatures.

hardpan—A hard layer of soil or ground that impedes the downward movement of water.

hardy—Capable of surviving unfavorable environmental conditions.

heat-zone map—A map that is zoned to indicate the average number of days a region experiences temperatures above 86°F.

heaving—An effect caused by the repeated freezing and thawing of soil.

hedgerows—Combinations of different plants planted in rows.

hedges—A grouping of the same plants grown in a row.

herbaceous—Nonwoody.

herbaceous plants—Nonwoody plants that have flexible, green stems.

herbaceous roots—Nonwoody roots.

humid—A moist atmospheric condition.

humidity—Invisible moisture in the air.

humus—Very dark end product of decomposition of organic material.

hygroscopic water—Moisture that remains as a thin film tightly bound to soil particles; not available for plant use.

incomplete fertilizer—A formulation that contains one or two of three standard nutrient elements of nitrogen (N), phosphorus (P), and potassium (K), but not all three.

infectious diseases—Diseases that are caused by living organisms.

inorganic fertilizer—Fertilizers derived from nonorganic sources, having neither a carbon structure nor a derivation from living matter.

inorganic mulch—Inert material used to cover large areas of soil such as gravel, crusher fines, black plastic, and synthetic fabric.

internodes—The portions of a stem (shoot) between buds (nodes).

irrigation—The deliberate application of water to a landscape or plants.

latitude—The distance north or south from the equator, measured in degrees.

lawn—A uniformly maintained turf grass consisting of thousands of grass plants tightly meshed together, appearing and acting as one.

leach—To remove soluble salts or contaminants from the soil profile.

leaf litter—Fallen leaves that remain on the ground.

loam—Medium-textured soil with a balanced mix of sand, silt, clay, and organic matter—the ideal soil.

macronutrient—A plant nutrient consumed in relatively large amounts such as nitrogen (N) or carbon (C).

macroorganisms—A general term for living beings that can be seen without the aid of a microscope.

maintenance—Keeping the landscape and plants well maintained and in a healthy condition.

mesic—Moist soil; moist conditions. Plants that require moist soil.

microclimates—Climates of localized spaces that differ from the overall climate of the area, such as under a tree or at the top of a hill or in between buildings.

micronutrients—Nutrient elements that are consumed in small amounts such as iron or zinc.

microorganisms—A general term for small, usually microscopic, living organisms such as bacteria, algae, protozoa, and nematodes that cannot be seen with the naked eye.

midday water deficit—At the hottest part of the day, many plants lose more water than they can extract from the soil, creating a water deficit and wilt.

mulch—Inorganic or organic materials used to protect the soil from erosion and excessive evaporation of moisture as well as holding down weeds.

mulch composting—Spreading dried, shredded material on top of the soil that slowly breaks down and gradually filters into the soil.

mycorrhizae—Special fungi that live in and around plant roots and act in symbiosis with plants to help extract water and nutrients from the soil.

native plants—Species that through thousands of years have evolved and adapted to specific environments and geographic regions; because of this, they are better equipped to tolerate the regional climate and local weather conditions.

natural communities—Natural associations among plants and animals that are part of the same ecosystem.

natural ecosystems—Ecological systems in which living organisms and nonliving elements interact to sustain the whole.

natural organic fertilizer—Nutrient elements derived from animal or plant by-products.

natural survival range—The range between a plant's maximum hot and minimum cold temperature tolerance.

needle evergreen—Plants with evergreen, needlelike to scalelike leaves such as pines.

needle leaves—Very thin, longer than wide leaves; resembling a needle.

nitrogen fixation—The conversion of nitrogen into nitrates or ammonia.

noninfectious diseases—Diseases caused by poor nutrition, temperature extremes, pollution, fluctuation in moisture, poor planting sites, and acid rain, among others.

nonorganic—Derived from nonliving components; without a carbon structure.

nutrient—Foods that provide nourishment.

nutrient elements—Elements that are necessary for nutrition.

organic—Associated with living organisms; having a carbon-based structure.

organic matter—Materials derived from organic substances.

organic mulch—Materials derived from plant or animal by-products, such as wood chips or manure, used to prevent erosion and evaporation and to inhibit weed growth.

ornamental grasses—Plants in the grass family with decorative features such as foliage, flowers, or form.

oxygen—An element required for plant and animal respiration; its presence in the soil is necessary for healthy root growth.

peat—Specific plants, such as moss, that grow in bogs; often used as a soil amendment.

peds—See aggregates.

perennials—Herbaceous or woody plants that continue to live from year to year.

pesticides—Legal poisons that kill infecting organisms by contact or by ingestion.

pH—The measure of acidity or alkalinity that defines the amount of hydrogen ions in the soil.

pheromones—Sex attractants that animals and insects secrete to influence the behavior of the opposite sex of the same species.

photosynthates—Sugars that are created by the process of photosynthesis; the basic materials for plant growth.

photosynthesis—A process by which plants use sunlight, carbon dioxide, and water to make simple sugars; essential for supplying energy and the building blocks for plant growth.

plot plan—An official record that usually accompanies the title deed, generally drawn to scale showing the outline of the house, driveway, and property lines.

prairie—Fairly level to rolling land dominated by grasses and dotted with wildflowers.

precipitation—Visible moisture that falls to the ground (rain, snow, sleet, or hail).

recycled water—Water that has already been used.

recycling—The process of reusing something.

relative humidity—The amount of water vapor in the air, expressed as a percentage based on how much moisture the air could hold at a specific temperature.

root hairs—Projections from the outer layer of cells of roots that come in direct contact with the soil.

root zone—The area in which the roots are growing.

roots—Plant organs that anchor the plant as well as extract dissolved nutrients and water for the plant's growth and development.

salts—Combinations of elements such as NaCl (table salt), KCl (potassium chloride), and KNO3 (potassium nitrate).

sand—Mineral particles that measure between 2 to .05 millimeters; can be seen with the naked eye.

scaly leaves—Small leaves that look like fish scales.

semiarid areas—Regions of low relative humidity and low annual precipitation (10 to 20 inches); vegetation ranges from shrubby to short grasses.

sex attractants (pheromones)—See pheromones.

shade tree—A large tree usually over 40 feet tall, with a wide, spreading canopy that provides shade.

shoots—The aboveground parts of the plant that bear buds, leaves, flowers, and fruits.

shredders and chippers—Machines that cut up leaves or break up woody material into smaller pieces.

shrub land—An ecosystem dominated by shrub growth; often transitional between other ecosystems.

shrubs—Plants with multiple basal stems that range in height from less than 1 foot up to 15 feet.

silt—Mineral particles measuring between .05 to .002 millimeters; can only be seen under a microscope.

slope orientation—Compass direction the slope faces.

slow-release fertilizer—Materials (natural or synthetic) that require microbial, chemical, and/or physical breakdown to become available to plants.

soaker hoses—Long, flattened hoses with small openings that allow small streams of water to soak into the soil.

sod—Grass-covered surface held together by matted roots.

soil—The earth's crust composed of mineral particles, dead and live organisms, air, and water.

soil drainage—The rate at which water moves through the soil.

soil profile—Defined layers dominated by different materials, starting with topsoil on down to bedrock.

soil texture—The characteristics of mineral soil based on dominant mineral particles.

solar energy—Energy derived from the sun.

solar radiation—Heat and light energy emanating from the sun's rays.

sprinkler systems—Mechanical methods for applying water in fans over a surface area.

stomates—The pores in leaves through which the plant obtains carbon dioxide for photosynthesis, oxygen for respiration, and loses water vapor through transpiration.

stress in plants—Disruption in the plant's physical processes and conditions, generally stemming from external factors in the environment, site, or landscape.

stunting—Dwarfing of growth.

style of landscape design—The way landscape elements are organized such as formal, informal, or natural.

subsoil—The soil layer that lies beneath topsoil.

subsurface or subsoil irrigation—Drip irrigation submerged 4 to 6 inches underground.

supplemental irrigation—The application of water to supplement natural precipitation.

sustainability—The ability to support itself; natural ecosystems are sustainable; man-made landscapes are usually dependent on human maintenance.

synthetic organic fertilizer—A fertilizer with a carbon-based structure, often having the same composition as natural organic fertilizers, but man-made.

taproots—A few main, large, deep roots that also have some smaller branching ones.

temperature—The measurement of heat or cold as determined on a specific scale such as Fahrenheit or Celsius.

tensiometers—Tubes filled with water, combined with a gauge that measures soil moisture tension.

texture—Design qualities that are based on the thickness, size, color, shape, and form.

thicket—A dense growth of shrubs.

tilth—The workability or friability of soil.

topography—The surface features of the land.

topsoil—The surface layer of a soil profile where most organisms and root growth live.

transitional zones—The areas between two different zones or regions; may exhibit characteristics of both.

transpiration—The loss of water vapor from plant leaves through their pores (stomates).

trees—Large plants that usually have a single trunk, although there are some with several trunks.

tundra—An ecosystem that exists above treeline and supports low-growing shrubs, cushionlike plants, lichens, and mosses.

turf—Low, dense vegetation that holds the soil together with matted roots.

turf grass—Turf that is composed of grass vegetation.

turgor—The pressure exerted by water in a cell that keeps a leaf firm and not limp.

unity in design—The aspect that provides harmony among the design elements.

utility lines—Electrical, cable, telephone, gas, or other lines that provide services to your home.

vine—A weak-stemmed plant that supports itself by climbing, twining, or clinging to another surface.

warm-season grass—Plants that thrive during the warmer part of the growing season.

water deficit—Water stress in plants that results from a deficiency in soil moisture.

water harvesting—Collecting or redirecting rainwater or snow for landscape use.

water stress—A condition that occurs when plant demands for water exceed the supply.

water table—The level below the surface of the soil at which the ground is saturated.

watering in—The process of watering plants after planting to ensure soil and root contact and the plants' establishment.

weather—The combination of temperature, precipitation, relative humidity, and winds at a given time and place.

weathering—The result of being exposed to the elements of weather.

weeds—Aggressive, prolific, exotic species that are opportunists and grow tenaciously in exposed soil.

wilt—Limp foliage or plant structure that indicates water stress or a lack of turgor in plant cells.

wind—Air in motion.

woody plants—Plants with woody stems that experience active lateral cell division to increase stem and trunk diameter.

xeric—Dry conditions, dry soil. Plants that adapt to dry soil.

xeriscape—A creative landscape designed for water conservation.

xeriscape principles—The sum of planning and design, practical turf areas, appropriate plant selection, soil improvement, mulching, efficient irrigation, and appropriate maintenance to achieve a landscape that conserves water and other resources.

Bibliography

American Water Works Association, *Xeriscape Plant Guide*. Golden, Colo.: Fulcrum Publishing, 1996.

Greenlee, John, *The Encyclopedia of Ornamental Grasses*. New York: Michael Friedman Publishing Group, 1992.

Keesen, Larry, *The Complete Irrigation Workbook*. Cleveland, Ohio: Franzak and Foster, 1995.

Kelly, George, *Rocky Mountain Horticulture*. Boulder, Colo.: Pruett Publishing, 1967.

Knopf, Jim, *The Xeriscape Flower Gardener*. Boulder, Colo.: Johnson Books, 1991.

Kourik, Robert, *Drip Irrigation*. Santa Rosa, Calif.: Metamorphic Press, 1992.

Kourik, Robert, *Gray Water Use in the Landscape*. Santa Rosa, Calif.: Metamorphic Press, 1988.

Robinette, Gary O., *Water Conservation in Landscape Design and Management. New York*: Van Nostrand Reinhold Co., 1984.

Springer, Lauren, *The Undaunted Garden*. Golden, Colo.: Fulcrum Publishing, 1994.

Winger, David, *Xeriscape Color Guide*. Golden, Colo.: Fulcrum Publishing, 1998.

Books by the Author

Weinstein, Gayle, *Deciduous Shrubs for the Rocky Mountains and High Plains States*. Denver, Colo.: The Shereth Group, 1999.

Weinstein, Gayle, *Deciduous Trees for the Rocky Mountains and High Plains States*. Denver, Colo.: The Shereth Group, 1999.

Weinstein, G. A., ed., *Ornamental Water Gardening: How and What to Grow*. Denver, Colo.: The Shereth Group, 1991.

Index

Note: italicized page numbers indicate figures; "t." indicates table.

Absorption, 10
Alder, 94, *94*
Algae, 94
Ammonium nitrate, 93
Annuals, herbaceous, 51
Apache plume, 39
Arborvitae, 83
Aridity
    and humidity, 9
Arid climate
    gardening, v
    and humid-environment plants, vi, *1*
    landscape ideas from nature, 14–15
    plant adaptations, 10, *10*
Aspen, 8, *8*, 46
Aster, *52*
Astilbe, 52
Average-low winter temperatures, 5

Bacterial fire blight, 112
Barley, as cover crop, 78
Base plan, 22
    adding elements to the inventory,
      24, *26*
    contour lines, *28*, 29
    defining the scale, 24
    inventory, 22, *23*, 24
    measuring elevations, 24–29, *28*
    measuring the site for, 24–30, *25*,
      26, 26
    photographic perspective, 29–30,
      29
Bedrock, 62
Beech, 52, 106
Beetles, 110
Bermuda grass, 56
Birch, 39, 106
Black roots, 112
Blue grama, 55, 56, 122

Brown soil, 69
Buckwheat, as cover crop, 78
Buds, 105
Buffalo berry, 94
Buffalo grass, 55, 56, 122
Bulbs, 32
Bunchgrass, 55
Burr oak, 39

Capillary water, 74
Cardinal temperatures, 8–9, 8t.
Chapparal, 50
Chippers, 84
Chrysanthemum, 3
Circulation patterns, 34–36, *35*
Citrus, 106
Clay, 65, 66, 70, 73
    and drainage, 73
    and irrigation, 119
Climate, *2*
    determining your local conditions,
      15
    and elevation, 12, *13*
    microclimates, 12, 30–34, *33*
    and plants, 12–14
    precipitation and humidity, 9–10
    solar radiation, 2–5
    temperature, 5–9
    and topography, 11–12
    wind, 11, *11*
Clover, 94
Coarse plants, 42–43
Coarse soil, 68
    adding amendments, 76
Cold injury, 7
Compost, 81, *81, 82*, 82
    and air, 83
    alternative methods, 84–85

    carbon, 83
    grass clippings, 82
    "green tea," 81, 126, *126*
    how to, 82–85
    and humus, 81, *82*, 84
    ingredients, 83–84
    layering the pile, 84
    leaf litter, 79, *79*, 82
    and moisture, 82–83
    mulch, 81, 84–85. *See also* Mulch
    mulching mowers, 85, *85*
    nitrogen, 83
    pH testing, 84
    pile and structures, 82, 83
    process, 81–82
    and shredders and chippers, 84
    as soil amendment, 76, 81
    and temperature, 82
    time required to become humus, 84
    turning the pile, 84
Conservation, v–vi. *See also* Water
    conservation
Contour lines, *28*, 29
Corn, 53
Cost estimates, 56–57
Cottonwood, 83
Cover crops, 77–78, *78*, 84
Cowboy's delight, *52*
Crabapples, 34, 106
Crambe, 52
Creeping hollygrape, 88, *88*

Deciduous trees, 32, 48–49
    in landscape design, 49–50, *50*
Decks, 36
Desert
    beauty of, 51, *51*
    soil, 52

Design. *See* Formal design, Informal design, Natural design, Xeriscape design

Digging
    drainage trench, 99, *99*
    planting hole, 100, *100*

Disease, 110, 111–112
    infectious, 111, *111*
    noninfectious, 111–112
    resistance, 113

Dormancy, 5
    grasses, 54
    sequential, 41

Drainage
    and clay, 73
    exercise, 72–73, *72*
    and planting, 99, *99*
    problems, 69, *69*
    raising planting area, 99, *99*
    and sand, 73
    tiles, 99, *99*
    trenches, 99, *99*

Drip irrigation, 121–122, *121*
Drought, 10, 73
Dry stream idea, 21
Dryland farming, 125
Dryness, 10
Dutch elm disease, 110

Eastern exposure, 32, *33*
Ecological landscape, 18

Elevation
    and climate difference, 12, *13*
    as gradient, 27, *27*
    as percentage, 27
    contour lines, 28, *29*
    measuring on your site, 24–29, *28*
    steepness, 27t.

Evapotranspiration, 117, *117*. *See also* Transpiration

Evergreens, 5, *5*, 49, *49*, *49*
    and soil, 62

Fern bush, 39

Fertilizer, 90, 107
    ammonium nitrate, 93
    analysis, 92–93
    burn, 90, *91*
    cautions, 90, 93, *93*, 94–95
    characteristics and use of, 90–92
    complete, 92, 95
    formulations, 93
    grade, 93
    incomplete, 92–93
    inorganic, 90, 92
    leaching, 91, 92, 94
    liquid, 93
    nitrogen, 90, *91*, 93, 94
    nutrient availability, 91, *91*
    organic, 90, 92
    and pH, 90, 91, *91*
    phosphorus, 93, 94
    potassium, 93, 94
    reducing need for, 93–95, *93*
    solid, 93
    and soluble salts, 90
    synthetic, 90
    timed-release, 93
    and urea, 92
    volatilization, 92
    when to apply, 95

Fescue, 54, 55, 122

Fine soil, 68–69
    adding organic amendments, 75–76

Fine-textured plants, 43, *43*
Flood/basin irrigation, 120, *120*
Food chain, 110, *110*
Formal design, 17–18, *18*
Forsythia, *40*
Freezes, 8
Furrow irrigation, 120, *120*

Gambel oak, 39, *40*, 46
Golden currant, *40*
Goldenrain tree, 43
Gradient, 27, *27*
Grass clippings, 82, 122–123

Grasses, 53
    Bermuda, 56
    blue grama, 55, 56, 122
    buffalo, 55, 56, 122
    bunchgrass, 55
    cool- and warm-season, 54, 122–123
    cool-season, 54–55, *55*
    corn, 53
    dormancy, 54
    fescue, 54, 55, 122
    grains, 53
    irrigation, 53, 54
    Kentucky bluegrass, 39, 53, 54–55, 122
    lawns, 53–54
    needle and thread, 52, *52*
    ornamental, 53, *53*
    prairie, 15, *15*
    ravenna, 52
    rhizomatous, 55
    rice, 53
    rye, 54, 78, 122
    in tundra, 52
    turf, 39, 53, 78
    warm-season, 55–56, *55*, 122–123
    water conservation tips, 122–123
    wheat, 53, 78
    Zoysia, 56

Grasslands, 15, *15*
Gravitational water, 74
Gray soil, 69, *69*
Gray water, 40, 126–127. *See also* Water conservation, Water harvesting

"Green manure," 77–78, *78*, 84
"Green tea," 81, 126, *126*
Ground covers, 56
Groundsel, 52, *52*
Grouping plants, 40–41, *41*
Growing seasons, 7–8

Hand watering, 120, *120*
Hardening off, 7
Hawthorns, 34, *40*
Heat energy, 2–3
Heat zones, 8

Herbaceous plants, 51–53, *52*, 56
    growing points, 103, *103*
    planting, 98
    roots, 104
    shoots, 105–106

Honey locust, 39

Humidity, 9–10
    and aridity, 9

Humus, 81, 82, 84
Hydroscopic water, 74
Hydrogels, 77, *77*
Hydrophytes, 12, *12*
Hygroscopic soil, 74

Indian paintbrush, 52
Indigenous plants, 44, 47

Informal design, 18, *18*
Insects, 110–111
    age of and controlling, 113
Integrated pest management, 113
Irrigation, 115. *See also* Watering
    plants
    anticipating, 116–117
    and automatic timers, 115
    considerations, 36–38, 38–39
    design tips, 39, *39*
    drip, 121–122, *121*
    drip, 79
    efficiency in lawn irrigation, 122–
      123
    evapotranspiration rates as a guide,
      117, *117*
    flood/basin, 120, *120*
    focusing on plant roots, 118
    furrow, 120, *120*
    grasses, 53, 54
    hand watering, 120, *120*
    measuring one inch of water, 118–
      119, *119*
    measuring soil moisture, 117, *117*
    and microclimates, 118
    observing soil moisture, 116, *116*
    only what is needed, 118–119
    and plant needs, 118
    rules, 115–119
    and saturated soil, 74
    and soil, 118
    sprinkler systems, 120–121, *121*
    subsurface, 122, *122*
    types of, 119–122
    watching for signs of water stress,
      115–116, *116*
    water conservation tips, 119, 122–
      123
    when plants need it, 117–118
    when to water, 115–117

Juniper, 52, 83

Kentucky bluegrass, 39, 53, 54–55, 122
Kentucky coffee tree, 43

Lawns, 53–54
    efficiency in irrigation, 122–123
    water stress, 122, *123*
Leaching of fertilizer elements, 91, 92, 94

Leaf litter, 79, *79*, 82
Lichens, 52
Light
    and cell arrangement, 4–5
    and growth, 3, 5
    and nutrients, 3
    and seasonal change and dormancy,
      5
Light freeze, 8
Lilacs, 34
Lindens, 106

Maintenance
    and natural design, 18–19
    and overgrown paths, 35, *35*
Manure as soil amendment, 76
Maple, 39, 52
    silver, 41
Measuring. *See* Base plan
Medium soil, 68
Medium-textured plants, 43
Mesic plants, 45–46
Mesophytes, 14
Microclimates, 12
    eastern exposure, 32, *33*
    evaluating , 30–34, *33*
    and irrigation, 118
    northern exposure, 32, *33*
    southern exposure, 32, *33*
    western exposure, 34, *34*
Moderate freeze, 8
Moisture probe, 122, *123*
Moisture sensors, 117
Mountain ash, 34
Mountain mahogany, 39
Mulch, 79, 84–86, *85*
    cautions, 85–86
    components, 85
    creeping hollygrape, 88, *88*
    decorative, 85
    defined, 86
    fabric, 86, 87, *87*
    how much to apply, 89–90
    inorganic, 86–88, *87*
    mulch composting, 84–85
    mulching mowers, 85, *85*
    organic, 86, *86*
    selecting, 88
    stone with cactus, 88, *88*
    types of, 86–88, 89t.

when to apply, 89
Mycorrhizae, 104, *104*

Native plants, 44, 47
Natural design, 18–19, *19*
    maintenance, 18–19
Natural environment, vi
Needle and thread grass, 52, *52*
New Mexican privet, 50
Nitrogen, 94
    in compost, 83
    in fertilizer, 90, *91*, 93
Northern exposure, 32, *33*

Oaks, 83, 106
Organic soil, 62, 69, *69*, 70
Ornamental shrubs, 34

Parklands, 14, *14*
Patios, 36
Pea family, 94
Peds, 70
Penstemon, 52
Percentage of elevation, 27
Perennials, herbaceous, 51–52
Pests
    alternative (integrated) manage-
      ment, 113
    biological controls, 113
    and crop rotation, 113
    defined, 110–111
    pesticide control, 112, *112*
    traps, 113, *113*
Phosphorus, 93, 94
Photographic perspective, 29–30, *29*
pH
    exercise, 71–72
    in fertilizer, 90, 91, *91*, 94
    in soil, 71, *71*
    testing in compost, 84
Pine, 83, 106
Piñon pine, 41, 52
Plant hardiness, 5–7, *7*
    zones, 5–6, *6*
Plant stress, 107
    acute, 108
    chronic, 108
    by disease, 110, 111–112
    ingredients of infectious disease,
      111, *111*

by insects, 110–111, *111*
signs of, 108
types of, 108
water stress, 108–110, *108, 109*
Planting, 97
    checking soil drainage, 99, *99*
    checking soil interface, 100–101
    digging the hole, 100, *100*
    and drainage tiles, 99, *99*
    and drainage trenches, 99, *99*
    effect of soil interface on plants,
        100–101, *100*
    first half of year, 97
    handling plants, 98, 101
    herbaceous plants, 98
    as plant establishment, 97, 98
    plant placement, 101–102, *101,
        102*
    process, 99–103
    raising planting area for drainage,
        99, *99*
    root growth, 104–105, *104, 105*
    and root regeneration, 97, 98
    second half of year, 97–98
    securing and staking trees, 102, *102*
    shading tree trunks, 103, *103*
    shoot growth, 105–106, *106*
    and soil, 98
    timing and temperature, 97–98
    and transpiration, 97
    trees, 98
    watering the plant, 102, 107
    woody plants, 98
    wrapping tree trunks, 102–103
Plants
    adaptations in arid and semiarid
        climates, 10, *10*
    adaptations to water deficit, 75, *75*
    and climate, 12–14
    coarse, 42–43
    colors, 42–43
    effect of soil interface on , 100–101,
        100
    as environmental controls, 42, *42*
    fine-textured, 43, *43*
    functions, 42–43, *42*
    grouping, 40–41, *41*
    growing points, 103, *103*
    growth, 103
    handling, 98, 101

herbaceous, 51–53, *52*, 56
humid-environment, vi, *1*
humid-environment plants in arid
        and semiarid climate, vi, *1*
indigenous, 44, 47
inventory, 48, 48t.
maintenance, 103
medium-textured, 43
mesic, 45–46
native, 44, 47
purchase, 56
roots, 104–105
selecting, 44–56
selection exercise, 47–48
size, 56
structure, 42, *42*
suited to existing soil, 78
textures, 42–43
watering, 102, 107
woody, 98
xeric, 45–46, 118
Plot plan, 21–22, *22*
Poplars, 106
Potassium, 93, 94
Prairie grasslands, 15, *15*
Precipitation and humidity, 9–10
Pruning, 107
Pygmy forest, 14

Rabbitbrush, 69
Ravenna grass, 52
Red soil, 69
Rice, 53
Roots, 104
    anchor, 104, *104*
    black, 112
    categories, 104
    fibrous, 104, *104*
    growth, 104–105
    hazards to, 105, *105*
    herbaceous, 104
    and irrigation, 118
    and mycorrhizae, 104, *104*
    regeneration, 97, 98
    and shoots, 107
    soil and growth, 64, *64*
    taprooted, 104, *104*
    transport, 104, *104*
    and water conservation, 122
    woody, 104

Rye, 54, 122
    as cover crop, 78

Sage, 41
Sagebrush, 52
Sand, 65, 66, 70, *70*
    and drainage, 73
Saturated soil, 68, 69, 74
Sedges, 52
Semiarid climate
    gardening, v
    and humid-environment plants, vi, 1
    landscape ideas from nature, 14–15
    plant adaptations, 10, *10*
Sequential dormancy, 41
Service paths, 35, 36
Serviceberry, 34
Severe freeze, 8
Shade, 3
Shade trees, 41
Shoots, 105–106
    annual growth spurts, 106
    biannual growth spurts, 106
    growth, 106
    hazards to, 106
    nodes and internodes, 105–106, *106*
    and roots, 107
    waves of growth spurts, 106
Shredders, 84
Shrub lands, 15, *15*
Shrubby willows, 52
Shrubs, 41, 56, 106
    broadleaf evergreen, 50
    in landscape design, 50–51, *50*
    ornamental, 34
    xeric, 46, 50
Silt, 65
Silver maple, 41
Site. *See* Base plan
Slopes, 3
    elevations, 12
    and exposure, 11–12
    as gradient, 27, *27*
    as percentage, 27
    contour lines, 28, *29*
    steepness, 27t.
Soil, 61–64
    adding amendments, 75–77
    bedrock, 62
    brown, 69

and chemical weathering of rock, 61, *61*
classification chart, 65, 66
clay, 65, 66, 70, 119
coarse texture, 68, 76
compaction, 76, *76*
components, 61
compost as amendment, 76, 81
and deciduous trees, 62
deserts, 62
drainage and planting, 99, *99*
drainage exercise, 72–73, *72*
drainage problems, 69, *69*
effect of interface on plants, 100–101, *100*
effects of construction, 62–64, *64*
evaporation and salts, 73, *73*
evergreen forests, 62
exercises, 64–68
at field capacity, 74
fine texture, 68–69, 75–76
gray, 69, *69*
for healthy plant growth, 75
humid areas, 62
hydrogels as amendments, 77, *77*
hygroscopic, 74
improvement, 75–78
improving by aeration, 78, *78*
improving with cover crops ("green manure"), 77–78, *78*, 84
inorganic amendments, 77
interface, 98, 100–101
and irrigation, 118
jar exercise, 65–66, *65*
and landscape, 74–75
and leaf litter, 79, *79*, 82
management, 79
manure as amendment, 76
measuring moisture, 117, *117*
medium texture, 68
mineral, 66
mineral particles, 65–66
moisture, 116, *116*
mulch, 79, 84–85, 85–90
nutrients and pH exercise, 71–72
nutrients, 71–72, *72*
organic, 62, 69, *69*, 70
organic amendments, 76
particle sizes, 65, 66
peds, 70

pH, 71, *71*
pinch texture exercise, 65, 65
and planting, 98
preserving and protecting, 79
professional testing, 72
profile, 62, *62*
profile exercise, 69, *69*
red, 69
and root growth, 64, *64*
sand, 65, 66, 70, *70*, 73
saturated, 68, 69, 74
selecting plants suited to, 78
silt, 65
structure exercises, 70, *70*
subsoil, 62
texture, 66, 68–69
topsoil, 62
and vegetation types, 62
and water, 73–74
workability, 66–68, *67*, *68*, 70
workability exercise, 66–68, *67*, *68*
world map, 63
and xeriscape design, 20, 34
yellow, 69, *69*
young, 62
Solar energy, 3
Solar radiation, 2–5
Soluble salts, 90
Southern exposure, 32, *33*
Southern pines, 106
Sprinkler systems, 120–121, *121*
Steepness, 27t.
Stomates, 10, *10*
Strawberries, 3
Stress. *See* Plant stress, Water stress
Subsoil, 62
Subsurface irrigation, 122, *122*
Sumac, 39

Tall fescue, 55
Temperature
    cardinal, 8–9
    growing seasons, 8
    hardening off, 7
    and plant hardiness, 5–7
    range, 3
    temperate zone, 8t.
    tropical zone, 8t.
    tundra zone, 8t.
Tensiometers, 117, *117*

Texture
    plants, 42–43
    soil, 66, 68–69
Threadleaf coreopsis, 52
Topography, 11–12, 34
    and exposure, 11–12
Topsoil, 62
Traditional landscaping, 9
Transpiration, 10. *See also* Evapotranspiration
Transplanting, 107
Trees, 56
    deciduous, 32, 48–49
    irrigating, 39, 49
    in landscape design, 48–50
    planting, 98
    securing and staking, 102, *102*
    shade, 41
    shading trunks, 103, *103*
    small, 34
    wrapping trunks, 102–103
Tropical plants, 106
Turf grass, 39, 53, 78
Turgor, 108, *108*
Twig dieback, 112

Urea, 92

Vegetative expressions, 1–2, *2*, *4*
Viburnums, 34
Vines, 32
    in landscape design, 51, *51*

Walnut, 43
Water
    capillary, 74
    gravitational, 74
    hygroscopic, 74
Water conservation. *See also* Gray water, Water harvesting
    design tips, 38
    tips, 119, 122–123
Water harvesting, 40, 124. *See also* Gray water, Water conservation
    capturing runoff, 124, *124*
    collecting in containers, 126
    from driveways, 124–125
    dryland farming method, 125
    from gutters and downspouts, 124, *125*

interspersing planters between hard
    spaces, 125, *125*
soil storage, 125
terracing, 125, *125*
trapping snow melt, 124, *124*
Water moisture probe, 122, *123*
Water stress, 108–109
    domino effect, 109, *109*
    in dry periods, 109–110
    in lawns, 122, *123*
    loss of turgor, 108, *108*
    minimizing, 109–110
    from overwatering, 108–109
    signs of, 115–116, *116*
    from underwatering, 108
Watering plants, 102, 107. *See also*
        Irrigation
    in dry periods, 109–110
    by hand, 120, *120*
    with water restrictions, 110
Weed control, 113
Western exposure, 34, *34*
Wheat, 53
    as cover crop, 78
White pine, 106
Willows, 39, 52
Wilt, 74, *74*, 75, 108–109
Wind, 11, *11*
Woodlands, 14, 15
Woody plants
    growing points, 103, *103*
    planting, 98
    roots, 104
    shoots, 105–106

Xeric plants, 45–46
    irrigating, 118
    shrubs, 50
Xeriscape, 127
    seven basic principles, vi–vii

Xeriscape design, 17, 127
    accent, 43, *44*
    accounting for seasonal changes,
        36, *36*
    aesthetic features, 42–43, *43*
    balance, 43–44, *44*
    base plan, 22
    base plan inventory, 22, *23*, 24
    conceptual design, 30–56
    connecting activities (circulation
        patterns), 34–36, *35*
    cost estimates, 56–57, 60t.
    deciduous trees, 49–50, *50*
    decks and patios, 36
    defining activities, 30, *31*
    drawing the final plan, 56
    earthmoving, 60
    eastern exposure, 32, *33*
    ecological considerations, 40–41
    elements, 41–44
    evaluating microclimates, 30–34, *33*
    evergreens, *49*
    extending outdoor views, 20
    formal, 18, *18*
    gathering ideas, 20–21
    grouping plants, 40–41, *41*
    herbaceous plants, 51–53, *52*, 56
    implementing the plan, 57–60, *57*,
        58, 59t., 60t.
    indigenous plants, 44, 47
    indoor/outdoor relationship, 19
    informal, 18, *18*
    initiating on paper, 21–30
    irrigation considerations, 36–39
    irrigation design tips, 39, *39*
    learning the basics, 21
    looking at soil, 20
    measuring the site for the base
        plan, 24–30
    native plants, 44, 47

natural, 18–19, *19*
    and natural ecological processes, 17
    northern exposure, 32, *33*
    outdoor/indoor relationship, 19–20
    plant functions, 42–43, *42*
    plant inventory, 48, 48t.
    plant purchase, 56
    plant selection exercise, 47–48
    plant size, 56
    plant structure, 42, *42*
    plant textures and colors, 42–43
    plants as environmental controls,
        42, *42*
    plot plan, 21–22, *22*
    refining the space, 36, *37*
    reviewing ideas, 30
    selecting plants, 44–56
    sensing the site, 19–21
    sequential dormancy, 41
    service paths, 35, *36*
    shrubs, 50–51, *50*
    simplicity and variety, 44, *44*
    soil, 34
    southern exposure, 32, *33*
    taking a break, 21
    topography, 34
    trees, 48–50
    unity, 43, *43*
    using nature as your guide, 46–47
    vines, 51, *51*
    visual relationships, 43–44
    and water conservation, 17
    water conservation design tips, 38
    western exposure, 34, *34*
Xerophytes, 14

Yellow soil, 69, *69*
Yucca, 41

Zoysia, 56